THE SOCIAL SECURITY CO-ORDINATION BETWEEN
THE EU AND NON-EU COUNTRIES

Social Europe Series, Volume 20

THE SOCIAL SECURITY CO-ORDINATION BETWEEN THE EU AND NON-EU COUNTRIES

Edited by

Danny PIETERS

Paul SCHOUKENS

Contributors

Rob CORNELISSEN

Klaus KAPUY

Grega STRBAN

Herwig VERSCHUEREN

Bernhard ZAGLMAYER

intersentia

Antwerp – Oxford – Portland

Distribution for the UK:
Hart Publishing Ltd.
16C Worcester Place
Oxford OX1 2JW
UK
Tel: +44 1865 51 75 30
Fax: +44 1865 51 07 10

Distribution for Switzerland and Germany:
Schulthess Verlag
Zwingliplatz 2
CH-8022 Zürich
Switzerland
Tel: +41 1 251 93 36
Fax: +41 1 261 63 94

Distribution for the USA and Canada:
International Specialized Book Services
920 NE 58th Ave Suite 300
Portland, OR 97213
USA
Tel: +1 800 944 6190 (toll free)
Tel: +1 503 287 3093
Fax: +1 503 280 8832
Email: info@isbs.com

Distribution for other countries:
Intersentia Publishers
Groenstraat 31
BE-2640 Mortsel
Belgium
Tel: +32 3 680 15 50
Fax: +32 3 658 71 21

The Social Security Co-Ordination Between the EU and Non-EU Countries
Danny Pieters en Paul Schoukens (eds.)

ISBN 978-90-5095-941-4
D/2009/7849/50
NUR 825

TABLE OF CONTENTS

PREFACE

On April 2nd, 2009 the Institute of Social Law of the K.U.Leuven and the European Institute of Social Security co-organised a conference on "The social security co-ordination between the EU and non-EU countries". The conference celebrated the 10th anniversary of the Master of European Social Security, organised at Leuven University.

The Master of European Social Security is an advanced one-year master programme organised by the Institute of Social Law of the K.U. Leuven providing a specialised, research based study of social security and this from a legal, social policy, administrative and philosophical perspective based on a strong comparative framework. The programme contains a multinational, multidisciplinary and comparative element as it focuses on social protection across Europe from different disciplinary angles. The content and educational approach of the programme aims at encouraging participants to engage in a profound scientific reflection on social security and to translate these scientific findings into relevant policy conclusions and plans.

Present book brings the various excellent interventions presented at this conference. In doing so this book sheds an innovating light on a topic of major scientific as well as practical interest that has seldom been dealt with in a comprehensive way. Outstanding speakers deal with the various aspects of the relation between EU and non-EU countries and nationals, as far as social security is concerned.

In a first contribution Dr. Rob Cornelissen of the European Commission deals with the internal co-ordination of the European Union in relation with third country nationals.

His former colleague and actual professor of the universities of Antwerp and Brussels, Herwig Verschueren, examines how the social security systems of the EU Member States are being co-ordinated with those of the Mediterranean emigration countries. He focuses in doing so on the Maghreb countries and Turkey.

Another kind of non-Member States of the European Union, are the European Free Trade Association countries. The EU-EFTA social security arrangements are explored by our former collaborator and actual legal counsel at the EFTA Surveillance Authority, Mr. Bernhard Zaglmayer.

Professor at the law faculty of Ljubljana, Grega Strban, gives an overview of the complex landscape of the existing bilateral and multilateral social security instruments binding EU states and non-EU-states.

Last but not least, our collaborator, Mr. Klaus Kapuy, writes about the European and international law and that very specific group of third country nationals, the illegal foreign workers.

The European Union is often inward looking; the same goes for European social security law. In this book we take another approach and we focus on the relations in the social security area between the EU and its Member States, on the one hand, and non-Member States and their nationals, on the other hand. We are very grateful to the various contributors to this book, to share their expertise in this important area of social security law.

Prof. dr. Danny Pieters
Prof. dr. Paul Schoukens

THE EUROPEAN CO-ORDINATION OF SOCIAL SECURITY AND THIRD COUNTRY NATIONALS

Rob Cornelissen*

1. INTRODUCTION: WHAT IS THE AIM OF CO-ORDINATION?

The Community Regulations coordinating the various social security schemes of Member States are based on Articles 42 and 308 EC. They are intended to ensure that people who make use of their right to free movement are not penalised in the field of social security. With this aim in mind the current Community Regulations[1] contain a large number of detailed provisions that, in the event of cross-border movement, aim to guarantee that:

- there are no conflicts of law, either positive (a person is insured in two or more Member States) or negative (a person is not insured in any Member State). Such conflicts are prevented by the provisions laid down in Title II of Regulation 1408/71, which contain uniform criteria for the determination of the applicable legislation. These rules have both an exclusive effect (a person is subject only to the legislation of a single Member State) and a mandatory effect (national affiliation conditions are overridden if their application is such as to deprive the conflict of law of all practical effect);
- persons covered by the Regulation are subject to the same obligations and enjoy the same benefits under the legislation of the host State as nationals of that State. Any discrimination-based on nationality, direct or indirect, is forbidden;

---

* Dr Rob Cornelissen is Advisor at the Directorate "Social protection and integration" of the European Commission in Brussels. This article only reflects the personal views of the author.

1 Council Regulation (EEC) 1408/71 of 14 June 1971, last amended by Regulation (EC)592/2008 of European Parliament and Council of 17 June 2008, O.J. L 177 of 4 July 2008 and Council Regulation (EEC) 574/72, last amended by Council Regulation (EC) 1791/2006 adapting certain Regulations and Decisions by reason of the accession of Bulgaria and Romania, O.J. L 363 of 20 December 2006.

- retention of rights in the process of being acquired: the mere fact that a person has completed periods of insurance or residence in two or more Member States should not result in that person not meeting the qualifying conditions for entitlement to benefits.
  To this end, Regulation 1408/71 contains a number of aggregation provisions[2]: the institution of a Member State whose legislation makes the acquisition of the right to benefits subject to the completion of periods of insurance or residence, has to take into account periods completed in another Member State as though they had been completed under its own legislation;
- entitlement to a benefit should not be lost or affected for the sole reason that the person concerned transfers his residence to another Member State. Therefore, Regulation 1408/71 contains a number of provisions[3] aimed at waiving residence clauses for entitlement to benefits in cash.[4]

These Regulations provide a high standard of protection in the field of social security for people moving between borders within the EU. At present, only people who are economically active (employed and self-employed persons) and students, together with members of their families or their survivors, are protected by the co-ordination system. The Community Regulations do not (yet) apply to non-active people.

2. SOME THIRD COUNTRY NATIONALS HAVE ALWAYS BEEN COVERED: MEMBERS OF THE FAMILY AND SURVIVORS. BUT THIS ONLY INVOLVES A LIMITED PROTECTION

Like its predecessor Regulation 3, Regulation 1408/71 applies to employed and self-employed persons (and to students) who are, or have been subject to the legislation of one or more Member States and who are a national of a Member State or who are stateless persons or refugees[5], residing within the territory of one of the Member States, as well as to the members of their families and their

2 Articles 18 (sickness and maternity benefits), 38 (invalidity benefits), 45 (old-age and survivors' pensions), 64 (death grants), 67 (unemployment benefits), 72 (family benefits) and 79 (family allowances).

3 Article 10 (for invalidity-, survivors' or old-age pensions and pensions for accidents at work, occupational diseases and death grants), Articles 19, 22 and 28 (for sickness benefits in cash), Article 73 (for family benefits), Articles 77 and 78 (for family allowances).

4 This 'export' of cash benefits does not apply to the so-called 'special non-contributory benefits'. For this kind of benefits, having characteristics both of social security and social assistance, a separate co-ordination system has been created: see Article 4 (2a), Article 10a and Annex IIa of Regulation 1408/71.

5 On the subject of stateless persons and refugees, see the Khalil judgment referred to point 4.

survivors, regardless the nationality of these members of their families or their survivors.

The objective of Regulation 1408/71 is limited to a mere co-ordination. It does not affect the freedom of Member States to organise their own systems. Member States continue to be free to determine the circle of persons which they consider as "members of the family". For this reason Regulation 1408/71 stipulates[6] that "member of the family" means any person defined or recognised as a member of the family by the legislation under which benefits are provided.[7]

However, members of the family and survivors cannot rely on the regulation as a whole. According to the Court, the Community legislature lays down two distinctive categories: workers on the one hand, and members of their families and their survivors on the other hand. In its judgment of 23 November 1976[8] the Court ruled that members of the family or survivors could only invoke the Regulation concerning derived rights: rights to benefits acquired through their status as members of the family or as survivors, such as family benefits, health care or survivors pensions. This was known as the *Kermaschek* principle and meant that members of the family or their survivors could not invoke the Regulation, unless it concerned benefits acquired through their status as members of the family. Twenty years later the Court refined its case law substantially. In its *Cabanis-Isarte* judgment[9] the Court limited the scope of the rule in *Kermaschek* to cases in which a member of a worker's family relies on provisions of the Regulation which are applicable solely to workers. In practical terms, it means that members of the family can now invoke the Regulation, unless it concerns provisions that are applicable solely to workers, such as the chapter "unemployment benefits". Members of the family can now, for instance, invoke the principle of equal treatment, laid down in Article 3 of Regulation 1408/71. Another example: where an employed person is subject to the legislation of a Member State and lives with his family in another Member State, that person's spouse is entitled, under Article 73 of Regulation 1408/71, to receive a family benefit such as child-raising allowance in the State of employment. The spouse cannot be refused such benefit on the basis of the distinction between a worker's personal right and the derived rights acquired by members of his family, since that distinction is relevant only where a member of a worker's family relies on the

6 Article 1(f) of Regulation 1408/71.

7 There is one exception: when a person needs health care while staying temporarily in another Member State, it is not the legislation of the Member State providing the benefit that decides who is to be considered as a "member of the family", but the legislation of the Member State where that person resides.

8 Judgment of 23 November 1976, case 40/76, *Kermaschek*.

9 Judgment of 30 April 1996, case C-308/93.

provisions of Regulation 1408/71, which are applicable solely to workers and not to members of the family such as those relating to unemployment benefits[10], and does not, in principle, apply to family benefits.[11]

3. NATIONALITY REQUIREMENT FOR EMPLOYED AND SELF-EMPLOYED PERSONS IN ORDER TO BE COVERED BY REGULATION 1408/71

The only persons who can invoke the Community Regulations as a whole are employed and self-employed persons (and students) who are nationals of a Member State, or who are stateless persons or refugees residing within the territory of one of the Member States. This means that employed and self-employed persons who are third-country nationals are, in principle, not covered by Regulation 1408/71. Why not?

The negotiators of the Treaty establishing the European Economic Community, signed in March 1958, considered the free movement of workers essential for the effective operation of a common economic market. Therefore, a number of provisions to ensure such freedom (Articles 48–51, corresponding to the current Articles 39–42 EC) were included in the Treaty. Free movement of workers means, in particular, that workers who are nationals of one Member State have the right to go to another Member State to seek employment and to work there. These workers have the right, if they so desire, to settle with their families in their new country of employment. They also have the right to be treated equally as national workers in the host State.

When the Treaty of Rome was drafted, its authors were fully aware of the differences between the social security schemes of the individual Member States. They had to ensure that the exclusive application of national law by the various Member States would not be an obstacle to the free movement of workers. This is why the EC Treaty includes a provision – initially Article 51 EEC and currently Article 42 EC – requiring the legislature to adopt such measures in the field of social security as are necessary to provide freedom of movement for workers.

In other words, the initial concept behind the coordinating Regulations was to avoid penalising, in the field of social security, for exercising or for having exercised their right to freedom of movement enshrined in Article 48 EEC (corresponding to the current Article 39 EC). Since only workers who were

10 Judgment of 25 October 2001, case C-189/00, *Ruhr.*

11 Judgment of 10 October 1996, conjoined cases C-245/94 and C-312/94, *Hoever-Zachow.*

nationals of a Member State enjoyed freedom of movement[12], it was logical at that time to reserve the protection offered by the Regulations based on Article 51 EEC (corresponding to the current Article 42 EC) to workers who were a national of a Member State. For this reason, Regulation 1408/71, like its predecessor Regulation 3, only applies to employed (and self-employed) persons who are nationals[13] of a Member State.

The exclusion of workers who are third country nationals from the scope of Regulation 1408/71 can lead to detrimental consequences, not only for the workers concerned but also for their employers. In fact, by virtue of Regulation 1408/71, workers who are temporarily posted by their employer to perform work in another Member State, continue to be subject to the legislation of the sending Sate, if certain conditions are fulfilled.[14] The provisions of Regulation 1408/71, which determine the applicable legislation, have an exclusive effect. This means that the worker is subject to the legislation of a single Member State only, namely the Member State whose legislation has been determined applicable by the Regulation. In other words: the institution of another Member State cannot claim contributions for a worker covered by Regulation 1408/71, who performs work on its territory but who is, in accordance with the aforementioned Regulation, subject to the legislation of the sending State.

It was exactly on the issue of posted workers who were not nationals of a Member State that the Court had to invoke the Treaty directly in order to counter the risk of paying double contributions. In fact, in its judgment of 3 February 1982[15] the Court ruled that Community law, in particular Articles 59 and 60 EEC (corresponding to the current Articles 49 and 50 EC) concerning free movement of services:[16]

> *'preclude a Member State from requiring an employer who is established in another Member State and temporarily carrying out work in the first-named Member State,*

12 Judgement of 29 October 1998, case C-230/97, Awoyemi, point 29.

13 Or who are stateless persons or refugees residing within the territory of one of the Member States. To understand why stateless persons and refuges have been included in the personal scope of the Community Regulations, see the Khalil judgment dealt with in point 4.

14 Article 14(1) of Regulation 1408/71. For a detailed analysis of the provisions of Regulation 1408/71 related to posted workers, see Prof Herwig Verschueren: "*Sécurité sociale et détachement au sein de l'Union européenne. L'affaire Herbosch Kiere: une occasion manqué dans la lutte contre le dumping social transfrontalier et la fraude sociale*", Revue belge de sécurité sociale 2006, 403–451.

15 Judgment of 3 February 1982, conjoined cases 62/81 and 63/81, *Seco.*

16 In its case law, the Court has underlined that Regulation 1408/71 not only aims at facilitating free movement of persons, but also freedom to provide services, see judgments of 10 February 2000, case C-202/97, *Fitzwilliam*, point 28, of 23 October 2003, case C-56/01, *Inizan*, points 21 and 25, of 12 April 2005, case C-145/03, *Keller*, point 46 and of 16 May 2006, case C-372/04, *Watts*, point 54.

using workers who are nationals of non-member countries, to pay the employer's share of social security contributions in respect of those workers when that employer is already liable under the legislation of the State in which he is established for similar contributions in respect of the same workers and the same periods of employment and the contributions paid in the State in which the work is performed do not entitle those workers to any social security benefits.'

Nevertheless, until 1994 Member States did not want to hear about an extension of the scope of Regulation 1408/71 to third country nationals. This changed after the Porto conference of November 1994.[17] During this conference, it was pointed out that it was not necessary to have exercised the right to free movement in order to invoke Regulation 1408/71. It was sufficient to be covered by the social security legislation of one of the Member States and for there to be a cross-border element. In fact, Regulation 1408/71 contains various provisions that fall outside the framework of freedom of movement. Article 22(1)(a) of Regulation 1408/71, for instance, guarantees that a German worker residing and working in Germany, who falls sick during a holiday in France, can receive medical care in France as if he or she was insured in France.[18] This also applies to the members of his/her family.

Following the Porto conference, the Commission submitted a proposal to the Council in June 1995 containing several modifications of Regulation 1408/71 (a so-called 'miscellaneous amendments' proposal). One of the modifications proposed was the extension of the scope of Article 22(1)(a) of Regulation 1408/71 to cover workers who are nationals of a third country.[19] The aim of this proposal was to address the most urgent problem, namely the provision of immediately[20] necessary health care to people insured in one Member State who are staying for a short time in another Member State. This part of the Commission's proposal was removed by the Council[21], when it adopted Regulation 3095/95.[22]

In November 1997 the Commission presented a proposal aimed at extending the scope of the whole Regulation 1408/71 to third country nationals.[23] However, this proposal foundered on its legal basis. Three Member States (DK, UK and Ireland)

---

17 'Social security in Europe-Equality between nationals and non-nationals', a report of the EU conference held in Oporto, November 1994.

18 The costs are borne by Germany.

19 O.J. C 242 of 19 September 1995.

20 At that time Regulation 631/04 modifying Article 22 (1) (a) of Regulation 1408/71 had not been adopted yet.

21 At that time The Treaty of Amsterdam was not in force yet. Under the Treaty of Amsterdam the Community Regulations can only be modified in accordance with the co-decision procedure.

22 Regulation (EC) 3095/95 of 22 December 1995, O.J. L 335 of 30 December 1995.

23 O.J. C 6 of 10 January 1998.

considered that, in view of the close link between Articles 48 (corresponding to the current Article 39 EC) and 51 (corresponding to the current Article 42 EC), the latter article could not provide a legal basis for extending the scope of Regulation 1408/71 to include third-country nationals. The dispute concerning the legal basis caused the proposal to be put on hold.

4. NEW POLITICAL AND LEGAL CONTEXT

Since the coming into force of the Maastricht Treaty, rules governing the conditions for entry, movement and residence of third country nationals were already 'matters of common interest' that could be addressed within the framework for cooperation in justice and home affairs.[24] But it was the Treaty of Amsterdam, in particular the incorporation of Title IV concerning immigration and asylum, into the EC Treaty that created a clear legal framework for third-country nationals.[25] In fact, the Treaty of Amsterdam inserted Article 63 into the Treaty, thereby providing specific Community competence to legislate on measures concerning immigration policy, as well as on measures defining the rights and conditions under which third-country nationals legally resident in one Member State may reside in another Member State.

Another important development was the introduction of the Charter of Fundamental Rights of the European Union, solemnly declared in December 2000 at Nice by the European Parliament, the Council and the European Commission. It enshrines a certain number of rights that are recognised with respect to nationals of the Member States as well as nationals of third countries who are legally resident in the Member States.[26] The *Gaygusuz* judgment[27] of the European Court of Human Rights put the discussion of the extension of the personal scope of Regulation 1408/71 to third country nationals into a broader legal perspective. In fact, in this judgment, the European Human Rights Court said that social security rights were property rights and that, accordingly, equality of treatment in social security is guaranteed by the European Convention for

24 For a detailed analysis of these provisions, see Helen Staples: "*The legal status of third country nationals resident in the European Union*", Utrecht 1999.

25 For a profound analysis of the importance of these provisions of the Amsterdam Treaty, see: Bergmann and Lenz: "*Der Amsterdamer Vertrag*", Köln 1998.

26 The charter has now been integrated into the Lisbon Treaty and has the same value as the Treaties. Article 6(3) of the new Treaty on European Union provides: '*Fundamental rights, as guaranteed by the European Convention for the Protection of Human Rights and Fundamental Freedoms and as they result from the constitutional traditions common to the Member States, shall constitute general principles of the Union's law*'.

27 Judgment of 16 September 1996, case 39/1995/545/631, *Gaygusuz* versus Austria.

the Protection of Human Rights. Further to this judgment, the question was raised in literature[28] of whether the exclusion of third country nationals from the scope of Regulation 1408/71 was compatible with the fundamental rights that form part of the general principles of Community law.

At its special meeting in Tampere in October 1999, the European Council created the pillars of a European immigration policy. According to one of the pillars, the European Union should ensure 'fair treatment of third-country nationals who reside legally in the territory of its Member States' and grant them rights and obligations 'comparable to those of EU citizens'.

On the other hand, the Court of Justice handed down an important judgment concerning the legal basis of Regulation 1408/71 in October 2001. In the *Khalil*[29] case, the Court was asked for a preliminary ruling on the question whether Article 51 EC provided a legal basis for applying this Regulation to stateless persons and refugees.

Mrs Khalil and her husband were Palestinians from Lebanon. Fleeing from the civil war in Lebanon, they arrived in Germany in the early 1980s where they have resided ever since. They were considered as stateless persons under German law. Their application for child benefits in Germany was refused because, by virtue of German law, only foreigners in possession of a specific residence entitlement or a residence permit were entitled to such benefits. Mrs Khalil and her husband claimed that, as stateless persons, they were covered by Regulation 1408/71, which would mean that they should be treated in the same way as German nationals with regard to the allocation of child benefits. Accordingly, those benefits should not have been made conditional on the possession of a specific residence document. Their appeal against the refusal of the German institution finally came before the *Bundessozialgericht* which decided to refer the following two questions to the Court of justice:

- Does Article 51 EC (corresponding to the current Article 42 EC) provide a sufficient legal basis to include stateless persons and refugees in the personal scope of Regulation 1408/71?
- If the answer to the first question is in the affirmative, does Regulation 1408/71 also apply to stateless workers and to members of their families who have travelled directly to a Member State from a third country and have not moved within the Community?

28 Herwig Verschueren: "*EC social security co-ordination excluding third country nationals: still in line with fundamental rights after the Gaygusuz judgement*?" in Common Market Law Review 1997, pages 991–1017.

29 Judgment of 11 October 2001, conjoined cases C-95/99 to C-98/99 and C-180/99, *Khalil*.

The Court answered the first question in the affirmative, but it was the grounds of the judgment that attracted most attention. The Court dwelt on the historical context of the inclusion of stateless persons and refugees in the personal scope of Regulation 1408/71. In fact, before the founding of the Community, Member States had entered into international obligations concerning stateless persons and refugees with one another and with third countries, not only under the treaties of Geneva in 1951 and New York in 1954 but also under the European Interim Agreements and the European Convention on Social Security for Migrant Workers of 9 December 1957, based on Article 69(4) of the Treaty establishing the European Coal and Steel Community. In view of this historical context 'the Council cannot be criticised for having ... also included stateless persons and refugees resident on the territory of the Member States in order to take into account the above-mentioned international obligations'. Otherwise, in the opinion of the Court, this would have meant that the Member States 'in order to ensure compliance with their international obligations, had to establish a second co-ordination regime designed solely for that very restricted category of persons'. It could be deduced on these grounds that Article 51 EC (corresponding to the current Article 42 EC) does not provide a legal basis for extending the Regulation to the very large category of third-country nationals residing legally in the territory of the Member States.

As to the second question, the Court recalled that the Treaty rules governing freedom of movement of persons cannot be applied to activities or situations 'which are confined in all respects within a single Member State'. In other words, Mrs Khalil, who was – as a stateless person – covered by the personal scope of Regulation 1408/71, could not invoke this Regulation since there was no cross-border element between at least two Member States.

In February 2002, all these developments caused the Commission to submit a new proposal[30] to extend Regulation 1408/71 to cover third-country nationals, this time based on Article 63(4) EC.[31] The proposal of 1997 was withdrawn at the same time. Although the Commission had no choice, submitting this new proposal was not without risk, for two reasons.

The Treaty of Amsterdam contains two protocols that are relevant to Title IV EC (which includes Article 63). Pursuant to the Protocol on the position of Denmark annexed to the Treaties, Title IV does not apply to Denmark. Neither does this Title apply to the UK and Ireland, unless these Member States decide otherwise in

30 O.J. C 126 of 28 May 2002, page 388.

31 In December 2001 the European Council of Laeken had already reached an agreement about Article 63 as the appropriate legal basis for a possible extension of Regulation 1408/71 to third country nationals.

accordance with the procedures laid down in the Protocol on the Position of the UK and Ireland ('opt-in or opt-out'). There was, therefore, a real danger that these three Member States, which had opposed the Commission proposal of 1997, would thank the Commission for submitting the new proposal to meet their objections ... and then decide not to participate in it.

Furthermore, it had to be seen how Parliament would react. In fact, since the entry into force of the Amsterdam Treaty, Parliament was now co-legislator for all legislation based on Article 42EC. However, as to proposals based on Article 63 EC, Parliament only had a consultative role.

In May 2002, both the UK and Ireland announced that they had decided to participate in the discussions on the Commission proposal, and that the legislation would apply to them, without requesting exemptions or special provisions.

The Commission was also able to convince Parliament that this proposal did not prejudice Parliament's future role as co-legislator under Article 42 EC. In fact, the proposal in question only had one substantive article: to make Regulation 1408/71 applicable to third-country nationals. Parliament would be able to fully discharge its role as co-legislator with regard to any future modification of Regulation 1408/71 itself. In addition, the Commission proposal would have as an effect that third-country nationals moving within the Union were given the same protection in the field of social security as EU citizens moving from one Member State to another. This was more than what had been requested by the European Council in Tampere ('comparable rights').

On 14 May 2003 Council Regulation (EC) 859/2003[32] was adopted extending the scope of Regulation 1408/71 to third country nationals. This Regulation was the first piece of Community legislation ever adopted under the new Article 63(4) EC.[33]

5. NOT ALL PROBLEMS SOLVED. WHAT DOES REGULATION 859/2003 MEAN IN PRACTICE?

Regulation 859/2003 offers third country nationals, in the field of social security, the same[34] protection as EU citizens moving within the Union. There are, however, two conditions.

32 O.J. L 124 of 20 May 2003.

33 Later more legislation was adopted on the basis of Article 63(4) EC: Council Directive 2003/109/ EC of 25 November 2003 concerning the status of third-country nationals who are long-term residents, O.J. L 16 of 23 January 2004.

34 The special provisions laid down in the Annex concerning family benefits in Germany and Austria only have a limited effect.

First of all, the person concerned must be legally resident in the territory of a Member State. This is the consequence of Article 63(4) EC constituting the legal basis of the Regulation. No Community legislative act defines what is meant by 'legally resident'.[35] Nationals of third countries who are legally resident on the territory of a Member State are the persons meeting the residence conditions laid down by the legislation of the Member State in which they are resident, and those who are authorised to reside there by virtue of a right arising from an act of Community law[36] or an international obligation contracted by the Member State in question or by the European Community, in particular in the context of association agreements.

The second condition is that the person concerned is in a situation 'which is not confined in all respects within a single Member State'.[37] In other words: there must be a cross border element between at least two Member States. A Lebanese worker, for instance, residing and working in Germany cannot invoke Regulation 1408/71 in order to claim the same amount of family benefits to which German nationals are entitled, if his children reside in Germany. However, if his children reside in another Member State, he can invoke Regulation 1408/71 because there is a cross border element between two Member States.

Is the requirement of a cross-border element between Member States met if the other Member State is Denmark? This is uncertain. Take as an example a third-country national, working and legally resident in Ireland. His children study in Denmark. Ireland refuses to pay family benefits for his children, since they do not reside in Ireland. It is, in my opinion, doubtful if the person in question can invoke Regulation 859/2003. The extension of Regulation 1408/71 to cover third-country nationals only applies to Member States that have adopted Regulation 859/2003 and this extension therefore only applies to cases affecting third-country nationals where the cross-border element is between these particular Member States.[38]

The condition that there should be a cross-border element between at least two Member States means that Regulation 859/2003 does not always guarantee that third country nationals residing legally in a Member State are treated equally as Community nationals in that Member State. In October 2007 the Commission

---

35 Other linguistic versions of Article 63(4) EC refer to a notion of 'stay' rather than 'residence'. Some examples: The German text: '...die sich rechtmässig in einem Mitgliedstaat aufhalten', the French text: 'en situation régulière de séjour dans un Etat membre', the Dutch text: '... die legaal in een lidstaat verblijven'.

36 For instance, Directive 2001/55 of 20 July 2001, Directive 2003/109 of 25 November 2003 and Directive 2004/81 of 29 April 2004.

37 Exactly the same wording as used by the Court in the *Khalil* judgment (see chapter IV).

38 This is reflected in recital 15 of Regulation 859/03: '*To achieve these objectives it is necessary and appropriate to extend the scope of the rules coordinating the national social security schemes by adopting a Community legal instrument which is binding and directly applicable in every Member State that takes part in the adoption of this Regulation*'.

presented a proposal[39] for a Directive, based on Article 63(3) EC, on a single application procedure for a single permit for third country nationals to reside and work in the territory of a Member State. This proposal formed part of the EU's efforts to develop a comprehensive immigration policy. One of the objectives of this proposal was to introduce a general framework for a fair and rights-based approach to labour migration. To this end, the proposal aims at guaranteeing a common set of rights to all third-country workers residing lawfully in a Member State and not yet entitled to long-term residence status. One of these rights is equal treatment in the field of social security compared with nationals of the host State. This proposal is, therefore, complementary to Regulation 859/2003, since it also covers situations that do not have a cross-border element between at least two Member States. This proposal is still pending before the Council.

Some categories of third country nationals already have an EU level guarantee of equal treatment in the field of social security, although there is no cross-border element between Member States. First of all, thanks to Directive 109/2003[40], third country nationals who have obtained the status of long-term resident in a Member State enjoy the same treatment, in the field of social security, as nationals of the host Member State. In addition, third country nationals who carry out a research project in a Member State enjoy equal treatment in the field of social security with nationals of the host State, thanks to Directive 71/2005/EC.[41] Finally, certain provisions of Association agreements concluded between the EU and third countries continue to have importance. Turkish workers, for instance, can invoke Article 3 of Decision 3/80[42] of the EEC/Turkey Association Council of 19 September 1980 directly in order to obtain equal treatment in the field of social security with nationals of the host Member State, even if there is no cross border element between two Member States. The equal treatment provisions laid down in the agreements concluded with Algeria, Morocco and Tunisia have a direct effect too, as the Court made clear in a number of judgments[43] which will be dealt with in the contribution of Prof Herwig Verschueren.

On this point, we have seen an interaction between the legislator and the case law of the Court. In fact, after the *Kziber* judgment of January 1991, the Council has refused to include an unconditionally-worded equal treatment provision in any association or cooperation agreement concluded with a third country.

39 COM (2007) 638 final.

40 Council Directive 2003/109/ EC of 25 November 2003 concerning the status of third country nationals who are long-term residents, O.J. L 16 of 23 January 2004.

41 Council Directive 2005/71/EC of 12 October 2005 on a specific procedure for admitting third-country nationals for the purposes of scientific research, O.J. L 289 of 3 November 2005.

42 Judgments of 4 May 1999, case C-262/96, *Sürül* and of 28 April 2004, case C-373/02, *Öztürk*.

43 Judgments of 31 January 1991 case C-18/90, *Kziber*; of 20 April 1994, case C-58/93, *Yousfi*; of 3 October 1996, case C-126/95, *Hallouzi* and of 15 January 1998, case C-113/97, *Babahenini*.

On the issue of equal treatment we should not forget, of course, recent developments in the case law of the European Court of Human Rights.[44] Mr Niedzwiecki and Mr and Mrs Okpisz were Polish nationals who had migrated to Germany during the 1980s. They were issued with limited residence permits there. Their requests for German child benefits were refused because, by virtue of German law, only foreigners in possession of a stable residence permit were entitled to such benefits.[45] The Polish nationals eventually brought their case before the European Court of Human Rights. They complained that the German authorities' refusal to pay them child benefit amounted to discrimination. They relied on Article 14 (prohibition of discrimination) in conjunction with Article 8 (right to family life) of the European Convention on Human Rights.

In both cases, the European Court of Human Rights ruled[46] that, according to its case law, a difference of treatment was discriminatory for the purposes of Article 14 of the Convention if it had 'no objective and reasonable justification', that is, if it did not pursue a 'legitimate aim' or if there was not a 'reasonable relationship of proportionality between the means employed and the aim sought to be realised'. However, States that have ratified the Convention enjoy a certain margin of appreciation in assessing whether, and to what extent, differences in otherwise similar situations justify a difference in treatment.

On the specific question whether the German law on child benefits violated the applicants' rights, the Court ruled that it did not discern sufficient reasons justifying different treatment with regard to child benefit for foreigners who were in possession of a stable residence permit on one hand and those who were not, on the other. The Court, therefore, held that, in both cases, there had been a violation of Article 14 of the Convention in conjunction with Article 8.[47]

Although the case law of the Court of Human Rights is not, as such, a binding source of interpretation of Community fundamental rights, it constitutes, none the less, a starting point for determining the content and scope of those rights within the European Union.[48] Taking that case law into account is, moreover,

---

44 See footnote 26.

45 Exactly the same reason for refusing the German child benefit as used by the German authorities in the *Khalil* case (see point 4).

46 Judgment of 25 October 2005, *Niedzwiecki vs Germany*, number 58453/00 and judgment of 25 October 2005, *Okpisz vs Germany*, number 59140/00.

47 In light of these judgments of the European Court of Human Rights, the German legislation on entitlement to child benefits has been revised in 2006 by the Law on the entitlement of foreigners to child benefit, child raising allowance and advance maintenance. The legislation is aimed at limiting the entitlement to child benefit to those foreigners who are likely to stay permanently in Germany. The question whether the criteria of the new legislation are proportionate to achieve this aim or not, taking into account the "certain margin of appreciation" of the Contacting Parties to the European Convention, has not yet been the subject of a decision of the European Court of Human Rights.

48 Conclusions of Advocate-General Poiares Maduro delivered on 9 September 2008 in case C-465/07, *Elgafaj*.

essential to ensure that the Union, founded on the principle of respect for human rights and fundamental freedoms[49], will contribute to extending the protection of those rights in Europe.[50]

6. LOOKING FORWARD. REGULATION 1408/71 WILL SOON BE REPLACED BY REGULATION 883/2004. WHAT ARE THE CONSEQUENCES FOR THIRD COUNTRY NATIONALS?

Regulation 1408/71 is on its last legs. In 1998 the Commission submitted a proposal to simplify and modernise it. After several years of negotiations, Council and Parliament adopted Regulation 883/2004.[51] On a considerable number of points, the rights of citizens have been improved by Regulation 883/04 as compared with Regulation 1408/71. The latter Regulation covers employed and self-employed persons and students, as well as members of their families. Regulation 883/2004 will apply to all EU nationals who are insured under national law. Inactive persons, for example, who are insured in a Member State on the basis of their residence there, will also be protected by Regulation 883/2004, if there is a cross-border element. In this way, the new Regulation strengthens European citizenship. The principle of equal treatment has been strengthened too, by the insertion of the important provision stipulating cross border recognition of facts or events.[52] Other improvements concern a variety of issues like cross border health care[53] and the introduction of the principle of good administration.[54]

The new Regulation 883/2004 is not applicable yet. A total of three Commission proposals need to be adopted by Council and Parliament before Regulation 883/2004 can become applicable:

---

49 Article 6(1) and (2) TEU.

50 Article 52(3) of the EU Charter of fundamental rights: '*Insofar as this Charter contains rights which correspond to rights guaranteed by the Convention for the Protection of Human Rights and Fundamental Freedoms, the meaning and scope of those rights shall be the same as those laid down by the said Convention. This provision shall not prevent Union law providing more extensive protection*'. See also footnote 27.

51 Regulation (EC) 883/2004 of the European Parliament and of the Council of 29 April 2004, O.J. L 200 of 7 June 2004.

52 Article 5 of Regulation 883/2004.

53 Article 20(2) of Regulation 883/2004 provides that when a person, who is insured in Member State A, seeks authorisation to go to Member State B to get medical treatment there, this authorisation must be given, if the treatment can not be given in Member State A within a reasonable time-scale from a *medical* point of view. This is in line with recent case law of the Court on cross-border health care (judgments of 23 October 2003, case C-56/01, *Inizan* and of 16 May 2006, case C-372/04, *Watts*). See also Article 28 which contains special rules for retired frontier workers and Article 18(2) concerning health care for family members of a frontier worker, which is an improvement compared with Article 20 of Regulation 1408/71.

54 See Article 76(4) and (6).

- Proposal for a new Implementing Regulation.[55] This proposal aims at achieving a more efficient and closer cooperation between the institutions. Exchange of information will happen by electronic means. The new implementing Regulation contains other provisions aimed at a smooth application of the rules, such as a set of provisions on the provisional application of legislation as well as on provisional granting of benefits.[56]
- Proposal for amending Regulation 883/2004 and determining the content of Annex XI.[57]
- Proposal for amending all the annexes of Regulation 883/2004.[58]

These proposals will be formally adopted by Council and Parliament very soon, which means that it is very likely that Regulation 883/2004 will become operational on 1 March 2010. Considerable progress has already been made and this justifies the expectation that Regulation 883/2004 will become operational in 2010. Regulation 1408/71 will be repealed from the date on which Regulation 883/2004 becomes applicable.[59]

It still is to be seen what consequences the replacement of Regulation 1408/71 by Regulation 883/2004 will have for third country nationals. One thing is sure: a new legal instrument is needed to extend the scope of the new coordinating Regulation to include third country nationals. On 23 July 2007, the Commission submitted a proposal to this end.[60] This proposal is still pending before the Council. From a strictly legal or technical point of view, this proposal should not cause too many difficulties. In fact, the proposal is more or less a copy of the 2002 Commission proposal which was adopted as Regulation 859/2003. However, it is a sensitive proposal from a political point of view.

There might be a problem linked to the fact that Ireland and the UK have to decide again, in accordance with the procedures laid down in the Protocol on the Position of the UK and Ireland annexed to the Treaties, whether to opt-in or to opt-out with regard to the new Commission proposal. Ireland has notified that it has decided to opt in. The UK, on the other hand, has not (yet) decided to opt in. If, indeed, the UK maintains this position, we could be faced with a rather complicated situation. In fact, by virtue of Article 90(1)(a) of Regulation

55 Proposal for a Regulation laying down the procedure for implementing Regulation 883/2004, COM (2006) 16 final.
56 Article 6, see Council document 8887/09 of 30 April 2009, SOC 261.
57 Proposal for amending Regulation 883/04 and determining the content of Annex XI, Com (2006) 7 final.
58 COM (2007) 439 final.
59 Article 90 of Regulation 883/2004..
60 COM (2007) 439 final.

883/2004, Regulation 1408/71 will remain in force and continue to have legal effect for the purpose of Regulation 859/2003 for as long as that Regulation has not been repealed (by the Regulation extending the scope of Regulation 883/2004 to third country nationals). Whatever the outcome of the current negotiations may be, I am convinced that the legislature will do its utmost to escape both of the following two scenarios:

- a step back in the protection of third country nationals: a category of third country nationals currently protected by the Community Regulations when moving between Member States being suddenly without protection when moving between the UK and another Member State;
- the new Regulation 883/2004 becoming operational while the old Regulation 1408/71 continues to apply in all cases involving third country nationals moving between the UK and another Member State.

7. CONCLUSIONS

For a long time workers who are third country nationals have been excluded from the high level protection offered by Regulation 1408/71. The extension of the scope of this regulation to third country nationals has only become possible after the incorporation of Title IV concerning immigration and asylum into the EC Treaty creating clear legal framework for third country nationals.

The adoption of Regulation 859/2003 has been an important contribution to the realization of one of the pillars of a European immigration policy: fair treatment of third country nationals legally residing in a Member State. In fact, Regulation 859/2009 offers third country nationals, in the field of social security, the same protection as EU citizens when moving within the EU. However, as the Court has underlined in its case law[61], the Community Regulations based on Article 42 EC do not apply to situations which are confined in all respects within one Member State. In order to invoke Regulation 1408/71 third country nationals have to demonstrate the presence of a cross-border element between two or more Member States. If they cannot, Regulation 1408/71 does not apply.

Some third country nationals do benefit from equal treatment in the field of social security, even when there is no cross-border element between Member States. The picture is rather complicated. First of all, third country nationals who have

[61] Judgements of 22 September 1992, case C-153/91, Petit, of 11 October 2001, case C-95/99, Khalil, and of 1 April 2008, case C-212/06, Walloon Government versus Flemish Government.

obtained the status of long-term resident do benefit from such equal treatment. The same is true for researchers. Turkish, Algerian, Moroccan and Tunisian nationals can invoke equal treatment provisions laid down in the association agreements concluded with these countries which have a direct effect, even when there is not a cross-border element between two or more Member States. But most other third country nationals still lack this protection. A Commission proposal aimed at guaranteeing equal treatment for all third country nationals who are not yet entitled to a long-term residence is currently pending before the legislature.

It still is to be seen what consequences the replacement of Regulation 1408/71 by Regulation 883/2004 will have for third country nationals. A new legal instrument is needed to extend the scope of the new coordinating regulation to include third country nationals. The Commission presented a proposal to this end in 2007. This proposal is currently pending before the Council. It is, of course, at this stage, premature to predict the outcome of the negotiations on this proposal. A number of sensitive issues play a role here. But I am confident that the outcome will neither constitute a step back in the protection of third country nationals in comparison with the current Regulation 859/2003 nor result in impossible complications for the institutions of Member States having to apply the new Regulation 883/2004, while continuing to apply the old Regulation 1408/71 in all cases involving third country nationals moving between the UK and another Member State.

SOCIAL SECURITY CO-ORDINATION IN THE AGREEMENTS BETWEEN THE EU AND MEDITERRANEAN COUNTRIES, IN PARTICULAR TURKEY AND THE MAGHREB COUNTRIES

Herwig Verschueren*

1. INTRODUCTION

Over the past decades a large number of nationals of non-EU Mediterranean countries have been spending shorter or longer parts of their working life in EU Member States. Most of them are still working or living in the EU and/or are entitled to social security benefits from EU Member States for themselves or for members of their families. Others have returned to their home States but continue to be entitled to social security benefits from an EU Member State.

Since the adoption of Regulation 859/2003 the internal EU social security co-ordination for these persons is dealt with by secondary EU legislation. This regulation extends the scope of Regulation 1408/71 to third-country nationals legally residing on the territory of a Member State and in a situation which is not confined in all respects within a single Member State.[1] However, the external co-ordination with the social security schemes of the countries of origin of these third-country nationals is not dealt with by secondary EU legal instruments. Such external co-ordination is in the first place subject to bilateral agreements concluded between the individual Member States and the countries of origin. Yet, with some of these states the EU has also concluded international agreements, containing provisions on social security rights of nationals of these states (and of the EU).

---

* Professor of International and European labour and social security law at the University of Antwerp and the Free University of Brussels. Herwig.Verschueren@skynet.be. This paper reflects the state of law on 15 April 2009.

1 Council Regulation (EC) No 859/2003 of 14 May 2003 extending the provisions of Regulation (EEC) No 1408/71 and Regulation (EEC) No 574/72 to nationals of third countries who are not already covered by those provisions solely on the ground of their nationality, *OJ* L 124, 20.5.2003, 1. See on this Regulation the contribution of Rob Cornelissen.

These Agreements co-ordinate, to a certain extent, the social security schemes of the EU Member States and of the third states. Some of these agreements are partially implemented, other implementation measures are still under discussion.

This paper analyses the provisions on social security rights in international agreements of this kind concluded between the EU and third countries of the Mediterranean, more specifically Turkey and the Maghreb countries (Morocco, Algeria and Tunisia). These international agreements establish special relations between the EU and the countries involved. Some of these agreements are called "Association Agreements", other "Euro-Mediterranean Agreements Establishing an Association" or "Stabilization and Association Agreements". Their overall objective is the establishment of special political and economic relations between these states and the EU, including also some social aspects of these relations, particularly with regard to migrant workers. These agreements contain several provisions on social security rights of nationals of both EU Member States and of the other contracting states. Furthermore they lay down procedures mandating institutions created within the framework of these agreements, to adopt more detailed rules on social security rights for nationals of these states when they move within them.

We will concentrate more specifically on the provisions with regard to social security in the agreements with Turkey (part 2) and with the Maghreb countries (part 3). Dating from as early as the 60s and 70s of the previous century, these provisions have indeed had the most tangible impact on the legal position of the migrant workers and the members of their families coming from third countries. Furthermore, they have been the subject of decisive case law of the European Court of Justice (ECJ) which, to a certain extent, ensures that these provisions have legal enforceability. Moreover, these agreements were implemented by decisions of the relevant bilateral Councils. A number of these implementing decisions have been proposed and are currently under discussion.

2. THE ASSOCIATION EEC-TURKEY

2.1. CONTEXT

The Association Agreement between the European Economic Community and Turkey was signed in Ankara on 12 September 1963 and concluded, on the Community's part, by the Council Decision of 23 December 1963.[2] In accordance

2 *OJ*, 29.12.1963, 3685.

with Article 2(1) of the Association Agreement, the aim of the agreement is to promote the continuous and balanced strengthening of trade and economic relations between the Contracting Parties, including in the field of labour, inter alia, by progressively securing freedom of movement for workers (Article 12 of the Agreement), in order to improve the standard of living of the Turkish people and to facilitate the accession of the Republic of Turkey to the Community at a later date (fourth recital in the preamble and Article 28 of the Agreement).

In Article 12 the Contracting Parties indeed agree to be guided by Articles 48, 49 and 50 of the EEC Treaty (now Articles 39, 40 and 41 of the EC Treaty) for the purpose of progressively securing freedom of movement for workers between them. In Article 9 the Contracting Parties recognise that discrimination on grounds of nationality shall be prohibited within the scope of the Agreement.

On 23 November 1970 an Additional Protocol was signed. It was annexed to the Association Agreement and concluded, on the Community's part, by Council Regulation 2760/72 of 19 December 1972.[3]

According to Article 36 of the Additional Protocol the freedom of movement for workers between Member States of the Community and Turkey shall be secured by progressive stages in accordance with the principles set out in Article 12 of the Agreement of Association between the end of the twelfth and the twenty-second year after the entry into force of that Agreement. However, the ECJ ruled in *Demirel*[4] that these articles essentially serve to set out a programme and are not precise and unconditional enough to be capable of governing the movement of workers directly.

On 19 September 1980 the Association Council adopted Decision 1/80 to implement Article 12 of the Agreement and Article 36 of the Additional Protocol. This decision did not introduce freedom of movement for Turkish workers in the Member States and it therefore does not encroach upon the competence retained by the Member States to regulate both the entry into their territories of Turkish nationals and the conditions under which they may take up their first employment. It merely regulates, particularly in Article 6, the situation of Turkish workers already integrated into the labour force of a Member State as a result of lawful employment over a certain period.[5] The rights guaranteed by Article 6, which are progressively extended in proportion to the duration of lawful paid employment,

---

3 *OJ* L 293, 29.12.1972, 1.
4 See the annex to this paper for the full reference to the judgements of the European Court of Justice to which it refers.
5 See, inter alia, *Kus*, para 25; *Tetik*, para 21; *Savas*, paras 27 and 58 and *Abatay*, paras 63–64.

are intended to consolidate the position of the person concerned in the host Member State.[6] Accordingly, a Turkish national's first admission to the territory of a Member State is, as a rule, governed exclusively by that State's own domestic law.[7]

However, this has not prevented the ECJ from recognizing in numerous judgements the direct effect of the provisions of Decision 1/80, in particular its Article 6 on the access to the labour market of the host Member State and Article 7 on the family members of Turkish workers.[8]

2.2. DECISION 3/80 OF THE ASSOCIATION COUNCIL

Article 39 of the Additional Protocol sets the Association Council the task to adopt, before the end of the first year after the entry into force of this Protocol, social security measures for workers of Turkish nationality moving within the Community and for their families residing in the Community. It specifies that such provisions must enable workers of Turkish nationality, in accordance with arrangements to be laid down, to aggregate periods of insurance or employment completed in individual Member States in respect of old-age pensions, death benefits and invalidity pensions, and also as regards the provision of health services for workers and their families residing in the Community. However, Article 39 explicitly confirms that these measures shall create no obligation on Member States to take into account periods completed in Turkey. Furthermore this article states that the measures adopted by the Association Council must ensure that family allowances are paid if a worker's family resides in the Community and that it must be possible to transfer to Turkey old-age pensions, death benefits and invalidity pensions.

On the basis of this requirement, the Association Council adopted, on 19 September 1980, Decision 3/80 on the application of the social security schemes of the Member States of the European Communities to Turkish workers and members of their families.[9] The decision applies to workers[10] who are, or have been subject to the legislation of one or more Member States and who are Turkish nationals as well as to the members of the families of these workers resident in the territory of one of the Member States and the survivors of these workers (Article 2). The

---

6 See *Günaydin*, paras 37 to 40 and 50.

7 *Savas*, para 65 and *Abatay*, para 65.

8 See for the first time *Sevince*.

9 This Decision was published in *OJ* C 110, 25.4.1983, 60.

10 Article 1 provides for a more detailed definition of "worker".

material scope with regard to social security legislation of the decision is identical to the material scope of Regulation 1408/71 (see Articles 4 in both instruments).

The aim is to guarantee Turkish workers moving within the Community the preservation of various social security rights, by analogy with the provisions of Community law concerning the co-ordination of national social security systems in favour of Community workers, as defined in Regulation 1408/71. Indeed by moving within the Community or to Turkey these workers could, on the basis of Member States' national legislations, risk losing certain rights. These provisions are also in line with the objective of the Association Agreement to progressively secure freedom of movement for Turkish workers *to* and above all *within* the Community (Article 12 of the Association Agreement).

Since the coming into force of Regulation 859/2003, the decision lost its relevance for the co-ordination of social security schemes of EU Members States in an internal EU cross-border situation.[11] However, it remains fully applicable to situations which are confined in all respects within a single Member State and for co-ordination with the social security schemes of Turkey. The equal treatment provision of Article 3 of Decision 3/80 is particularly relevant for the first situations.

A great number of provisions of Decision 3/80 refer to several (not all) provisions of Regulation 1408/71 as being applicable to Turkish workers employed in the Community. These provisions contain co-ordination mechanisms such as the determination of the applicable legislation as well as mechanisms for the different benefits in situations where more than one Member State is involved. However, since these provisions only apply to co-ordination of schemes of the Member States, they do not seem to be relevant any more after the adoption of Regulation 859/2003 (except for Denmark).

On 8 February 1983 the Commission presented a proposal for a Council Regulation implementing Decision 3/80 within the Community[12], but this Decision was never adopted by the Council. The proposed text of the Commission is comparable to provisions of Regulation 574/72 (which implements Regulation 1408/71) and would fulfil a comparable role, once adopted.

---

11 Except for the relations with Denmark, since this Member State did not take part in the adoption of Regulation 859/2003.

12 *OJ* C 110, 25.4.1983, 1.

2.3. THE LEGAL MEANING OF DECISION 3/80

In *Taflan-Met* (10 September 1996) the ECJ examined whether this Decision had effectively entered into force and was effectively binding on the parties. The Court confirmed that it follows from the provisions of the Association Agreement that decisions of the Association Council are measures adopted by a body provided for by the Association Agreement and empowered to take decisions. The decisions adopted by this body must implement the objectives set by the Association Agreement and have the effect of binding the Contracting Parties. By virtue of the Association Agreement the parties have agreed to be bound by such decisions. The binding effect of such decisions cannot depend on whether implementing measures have or have not been adopted. The Court ruled that, in the absence of any provision on the Decision's entry into force, it follows from the binding character which the Association Agreement attaches to Decision 3/80 that it entered into force on the date on which it was adopted, namely 19 September 1980, and that the Contracting Parties have been bound by the Decision since that date.[13]

This position opened the way for an examination concerning the direct effect of the provisions of Decision 3/80 at issue in *Taflan-Met*, Articles 12 and 13. Article 12 lays down the conditions under which the worker concerned is entitled to invalidity benefits if he has been successively or alternately subject to the legislation of two or more Member States. Article 12 refers in this connection to the provisions governing this matter in Regulation 1408/71. Article 13 stipulates that the rights to old-age and survivors' pensions of a worker or of his survivors (family members), who has been subject to the legislation of two or more Member States, shall be established in accordance with the provisions of Regulation 1408/71, which are specified.

The examination of the direct effect of the provisions of Decisions 3/80 was carried out in the light of the Court's jurisprudence concerning the direct effect, if any, of the legislation established within the framework of the association with Turkey. Thus, in *Demirel* the Court had considered that "*A provision in an agreement concluded by the Community with non-member countries must be regarded as being directly applicable when, regard being had to its wording and the purpose and nature of the agreement itself, the provision contains a clear and precise obligation which is not subject, in its implementation or effects, to the adoption of any subsequent measure*".[14] In *Sevince*[15] the Court added that the same criteria apply

13 *Taflan-Met*, paras 17–21.
14 *Demirel*, para 14.
15 *Sevince*, para 15.

in determining whether the provisions of a decision of the Council of Association can have direct effect.[16]

After examining the provisions in question the Court concluded in *Taflan-Met* that Articles 12 and 13 of Decision 3/80 cannot have any direct effect within the territory of the Member States as long as the Council has not taken the necessary measures to implement Decision 3/80 (as proposed by the Commission in 1983). The ECJ referred to the implementation by Regulation 574/72 of the relevant provisions of Regulation 1408/71 on rules concerning aggregation of periods completed in different Member States and non-overlapping of benefits paid by different competent institutions. In the absence of such implementing measures as proposed by the Commission, but not yet adopted by the Association Council, Article 12 and 13 of the Decision can not have any direct effect.

However, in *Taflan-Met* the Court took a very ambiguous position by stating that even though some of the provisions of Decision 3/80 are clear and precise, the Decision cannot be applied as long as supplementary implementing measures have not been adopted by the Council.[17]

Therefore the question arose as to whether the ruling in *Taflan-Met* applied to all the provisions of Decision 3/80, or whether some of these provisions were required to satisfy the criteria of the Court's case law in order for them to have a direct effect. The issue that immediately sprang to mind was the non-discrimination provision in Article 3.

2.4. THE DIRECT EFFECT OF ARTICLE 3 OF DECISION 3/80

In its judgement of 4 May 1999 in the *Sürül* case the Court of Justice ruled for a second time on the scope of Decision 3/80. The case specifically dealt with the principle of non-discrimination on grounds of nationality, based on Article 3 of this Decision.

The question regarding the applicability of this Decision arose as a result of the German legislation which, ever since it was amended on 1 January 1994, stipulates that foreign nationals living in Germany are not entitled to family allowances unless they hold a residence entitlement (*Aufenthaltsberechtigung*) or residence permit (*Aufenthaltserlaubnis*). On this basis the Sürüls, a married Turkish couple, were refused entitlement to a family allowance since, although lawfully resident

16 See also judgement in *Kus* and a large number of subsequent judgements.
17 *Taflan-Met*, para 37.

in Germany, they merely had a residence document issued for a limited period (*Aufenthaltsbewilligung*). The questions referred by the German court to the Court of Justice for a preliminary ruling concerned the applicability of Article 3 of Decision 3/80 and the personal scope of that Article. In the latter context, the German court wondered whether Mr or Mrs Sürül had the status of worker within the meaning of Article 2 of the Decision.[18]

The provision in question, Article 3 of Decision 3/80, is identical to Article 3(1) of Regulation 1408/71, and reads as follows: "*Subject to the special provisions of this Decision, persons resident in the territory of one of the Member States to whom this Decision applies shall be subject to the same obligations and enjoy the same benefits under the legislation of any Member State as the nationals of that State*". The material scope of this Decision is the same as that of Regulation 1408/71 (see Article 4 of both texts) and covers the traditional branches of social security.

In its judgement the Court first of all made a distinction between the prohibition of discrimination on grounds of nationality in Article 3 of Decision 3/80 and the provisions that were at issue in *Taflan-Met*, namely Articles 12 and 13. These latter articles required the adoption of implementing measures by the Council before they could have effect within the territory of the Community. The technical problems with regard to the implementation first needed to be resolved by the legislator. The Court therefore clarified the question that it had answered ambiguously in *Taflan-Met*, namely that in principle the direct effect of provisions of Decision 3/80 must not be excluded.

Once this basic obstacle had been surmounted, the path was clear for the Court to proceed with its now traditional testing of the provision at issue against the criteria for direct effect already established in respect of agreements concluded by the Community with third countries, including the decisions adopted by the EEC-Turkey Association Council. According to this case law, in order to have direct effect the provision must be one that contains a clear and precise obligation which is not subject, in its implementation or effects, to the adoption of any subsequent measure.[19]

The Court had no doubt whatsoever that Article 3 of Decision 3/80 satisfies these criteria. Referring to the argument put forward by the European Commission, the Court states that the rule of equal treatment lays down a precise obligation of

18 This paper will not dwell on this second question, namely that of the personal scope of the Decision, since this is a highly technical legal question pertaining to German social security law, the relevance of which outside the specific case is rather limited (see paragraphs 75–95 of the judgement).

19 *Sürül*, para 60 and the reference there to *Demirel* and *Kziber*.

result and, by its nature, can be relied on by an individual before a national court without any further implementing measures being required for this.[20]

This finding is supported, according to the Court, by the fact that Article 3 of Decision 3/80 merely constitutes the implementation and the concrete expression, in the particular field of social security, of the general principle of non-discrimination on grounds of nationality laid down in Article 9 of the Association Agreement (see more on this below under 2.6). Additionally, the direct effect is in keeping with the purpose and nature of the Association Agreement itself, namely the progressive achievement of freedom of movement for workers with a view to improving the standard of living of the Turkish people and facilitating Turkey's accession to the Community at a later date.[21]

Nor, according to the Court, is the foregoing interpretation invalidated by the fact that Article 3 states that the principle of non-discrimination applies only "*subject to the special provisions of this Decision*". This only signifies that an exception to the principle may be laid down in a special provision, but that the exception must be expressly stated. We could mention for example the Annex to the Decision, under which certain specified benefits are excluded from the scope of the Decision.[22] The principle of non-discrimination does not apply to these benefits.

However, apart from the benefits explicitly excluded from the scope of Decision 3/80, its material scope, including for the implementation of the equal treatment provision, is very broad. Its Article 4 is indeed identical to the version of Article 4 of Regulation 1408/71 at the time of the adoption of Decision 3/80, encompassing a wide range of social security benefits.

2.5. SIGNIFICANCE OF THE PRINCIPLE OF NON-DISCRIMINATION CONTAINED IN ARTICLE 3 OF DECISION 3/80

Once having established that Article 3 of Decision 3/80 has direct effect, the Court examined in *Sürül* whether the fact of requiring a Turkish national residing lawfully in the territory of a Member State to hold a certain type of residence document in order to be entitled to receive family allowances, is compatible with

20 *Sürül*, para 63.
21 *Sürül*, para 70.
22 Such as the Belgian Guaranteed Income for Retired People or the allowances paid by this Member State to handicapped persons and the French Supplementary allowance of the National Mutual Aid Fund. This list, however, has never been updated, including therefore benefits which possibly do not exist any more.

the prohibition of discrimination on grounds of nationality. In its analysis the Court uses the criteria traditionally employed regarding the principle of non-discrimination on grounds of nationality in Community legislation, either in primary legislation or in the Agreements with third countries.[23]

Turkish nationals covered by Decision 3/80 must be treated in the same way as nationals of the host Member State, which means that the legislation of that Member State cannot impose upon such a Turkish national more or stricter conditions than those applicable to its own nationals.

In *Sürül* the Court quickly came to the conclusion that the requirement imposed on aliens to possess a residence entitlement or residence permit, constitutes unequal treatment on grounds of nationality, because the only requirement imposed on Germans is that they be domiciled or habitually resident in the territory.

The Court in fact confirmed that the various different provisions in Community law (including the Agreements with third countries) concerning prohibition of discrimination on grounds of nationality must be interpreted in the same way.

This has been confirmed by subsequent case law of the ECJ. More recently in *Kocak and Örs* (14 March 2000), for instance, the ECJ ruled that as regards the scope of the principle of non-discrimination on grounds of nationality embodied in Article 3(1) of Decision 3/80, the rule of equal treatment prohibits not only overt discrimination based on nationality but also all covert forms of discrimination which, by applying other distinguishing criteria, achieve in practice the same result.[24]

The same principles were again confirmed in *Öztürk* (28 April 2004). This case concerned the refusal of the Austrian pension fund to grant Mr Öztürk an early old-age pension in the event of unemployment on the ground that, during the 15

---

23 *Sürül*, para 97.

24 *Kocak and Örs*, para 39. In this case however the ECJ came to the conclusion that Article 3(1) of Decision 3/80 does not preclude a Member State from applying to Turkish workers legislation which, for the purposes of awarding a retirement pension, takes as the conclusive date of birth the one given in the first declaration made by the person concerned to a social security authority in that Member State and allows another date of birth to be taken into account only if a document is produced of which the original was issued before that declaration was made (para 55). The Court refused to take into account the legal and factual differences between the German and Turkish legislation on birth certificates, which would make it possible to conclude that a refusal in principle to take account, for pension insurance purposes, of a date of birth other than that indicated in the first declaration made to a social security authority, constitutes a form of indirect discrimination against Turkish migrant workers.

months immediately preceding the qualifying date, he had not received unemployment benefit in Austria but in another Member State (Germany).

In its judgement the ECJ first confirms that the scope of Article 3 of Decision 3/80 is not limited to the Member State of residence. Its obligation to equal treatment also attaches to the other Member States in which a Turkish national has acquired social security rights or completed periods of insurance, residence or employment. Subsequently the ECJ called to mind that the rule of equal treatment prohibits not only overt discrimination based on nationality but also all covert forms of discrimination. Consequently, the ECJ considered the requirement of having benefited from Austrian unemployment insurance for a certain period prior to the qualifying date, which that legislation imposes as a precondition for entitlement to an early old-age pension, can be more easily fulfilled by Austrian workers than by Turkish migrant workers who have worked in Austria. It therefore constitutes an indirect discrimination on grounds of nationality. The ECJ did not accept the arguments of the Austrian institution that this is an issue of aggregation of periods, for which, according to *Taflan*-Met, Decision 3/80 has no direct effect. Nor did it accept the justification that this benefit must be seen as a social-protection measure for the benefit of unemployed people, in the context of the employment situation in the Member State concerned.[25]

Remarkably this ruling also means an important step in the evolution of the general interpretation of the principle of prohibition of discrimination on grounds of nationality under EC law. This principle implies, according to these developments in the ECJ's case law, also the principle of equal treatment of benefits, income, facts or events which has now been explicitly integrated in Article 5 of Regulation 883/2004. The judgement in *Öztürk* therefore not only builds on the case law applying the non-discrimination principle to EU migrant workers, but also demonstrates that the application of this principle under Decision 3/80 can, in its turn, contribute to the development of the general principle of non-discrimination in Community law.

2.6. SIGNIFICANCE OF ARTICLE 9 OF THE ASSOCIATION AGREEMENT

In *Sürül* the Court explicitly refered to Article 9 of the Association Agreement, affirming that this provision contains a general prohibition of discrimination on grounds of nationality, of which Article 3 of Decision 3/80 constitutes merely the implementation and the concrete expression in the particular field of social

[25] *Öztürk*, paras 62–67.

security.[26] The ECJ later confirmed that Article 9 of the Association Agreement is applicable without prejudice to any special provisions which may be laid down by the Association Council. This means that Article 9 of that agreement does not apply independently if the Association Council has adopted a specific non-discrimination rule, such as Article 3(1) of Decision 3/80 in the particular field of social security.[27]

Apart from that, Article 9 makes reference to what was at the time Article 7 of the EC Treaty (subsequently became Article 6 EC and is now Article 12 EC). The Court in fact ascribes to Article 9 of the Association Agreement the same role, in the context of the "Association law" as to Article 6 EC (now Article 12 EC). Any person covered by this Agreement can rely on the principle of non-discrimination insofar as the rights at issue fall within the material scope of the Agreement. This could be the case, inter alia, for workers not covered by the definition of "worker" in Decision 3/80 but covered by the more general definition of worker in the Association Agreement, Article 12 of which refers to Article 39 of the EC Treaty.

As regards the freedom of establishment and the freedom to provide services, the Contracting Parties agreed in the Association Agreement (Article 13 and 14) to be guided by the relevant Articles in the EEC Treaty for the purpose of abolishing restrictions on freedom of establishment and the freedom to provide services between them. However, the ECJ already had the opportunity to confirm that these provisions or those adopted in their context, such as Article 41(1) of the Additional Protocol, are not, in themselves, capable of conferring on Turkish nationals – on the basis of Community legislation alone – a right of establishment or, as a corollary, a right of residence, nor a right to freedom to provide services or to enter the territory of a Member State.[28] However the ECJ did not exclude that Turkish self-employed persons or Turkish service providers may invoke direct applicable provisions such as the standstill clause set out in Article 41(1) of the Additional Protocol. For the Court this provision has direct effect and may be relied on before the courts of the Member States.[29] Furthermore, the ECJ recognised that workers who are employed by an undertaking established in Turkey that lawfully provides services in a Member State, may invoke direct applicable provisions such as the standstill clause set out in Article 41(1) of the Additional Protocol on the ground that the employees of the provider of services are indispensable to enable him to provide his services.[30]

---

26 *Sürül*, para 64.

27 See, to that effect, *Kocak and Örs*, para 36 and *Öztürk*, para 48.

28 See *Savas*, paras 64 and 71; *Abatay*, para 62; *Tum and Dari*, para 52 and *Soysal*, para 47.

29 See *Savas*, paras 46 to 54 and 71; *Abatay*, paras 58, 59 and 117 and *Tum and Dari*, para 46.

30 See *Savas*, paras 69 and 71; *Abatay*, paras 106 and 117; *Tum and Dari*, paras 49 and 53 and *Soysal*, paras 46–47.

It remains unclear whether one could draw the conclusion from this case law that self-employed persons and service providers active in a Member State, may invoke Article 9 of the Association Agreement in order to apply for equal treatment with the nationals of the hosting Members State with regard to social security rights. Further jurisprudence would appear to be necessary to provide a definitive answer to this question.

2.7. POSSIBLE DIRECT EFFECT OF OTHER PROVISIONS OF DECISION 3/80, IN PARTICULAR THE PRINCIPLE OF EXPORT OF BENEFITS OF ITS ARTICLE 6

As explained above, the chief significance of *Sürül* and the subsequent case law lies in the recognition by the Court of the possibility, in principle, of the provisions of Decision 3/80 having direct effect. A provision must be regarded as having direct effect when it contains a clear and precise obligation which is not subject, in its implementation or effects, to the adoption of any subsequent measure. The question that can justifiably be asked, therefore, is whether any other provisions of Decision 3/80 can be considered to have direct effect. In paragraph 58 of *Sürül* the Court indicates the types of provisions which cannot have direct effect, including rules on the aggregation of periods completed in different Member States, the non-overlapping of benefits paid by different competent institutions and the determination of the applicable national legislation. An indication of the types of provisions that require further measures in order to have direct effect can also be found in the Commission's 1983 proposal for a Regulation implementing Decision 3/80 within the Community (see above). It appears from this that most of the provisions in the Decision require further implementing measures.

An initial examination of the provisions of Decision 3/80 to assess which of them might have direct effect points to one important provision that could satisfy the conditions imposed for direct effect, namely the waiving of the residence clause or the principle of the exportability of benefits (Article 6 of Decision 3/80). Article 6 stipulates that "*... invalidity, old-age or survivors' cash benefits and pensions for accidents at work or occupational diseases, acquired under the legislation of one or more Member States, shall not be subject to any reduction, modification, suspension, withdrawal or confiscation by reason of the fact that the recipient resides in Turkey or in the territory of a Member State other than that in which the institution responsible for payment is situated*". This provision is the same as that of Article 10 of Regulation 1408/71.

In the above-mentioned Commission's proposal for the implementation of Decision 3/80 no implementing measure is proposed for Article 6, and nor does Regulation 574/72 contain any special provision for implementing Article 10 of Regulation 1408/71. It seems, therefore, that for the payment of benefits to someone residing in Turkey or in another Member State no further measure is required from the competent legislator, and thus the provision has direct effect. This also seems to be in line with the mandate in the Additional Protocol.

Moreover, this conclusion does not conflict with the purpose and nature of the Association Agreement as formulated by the Court in paragraph 70 of *Sürül*, namely the development of trade and economic relations between Turkey and the Member States through the progressive achievement of freedom of movement for workers with a view to improving the standard of living of the Turkish people. This last objective in particular seems important in the context of the export of benefits. If a Turkish national can lose his right to receive a benefit on the grounds that he does not reside, or no longer resides, in the territory of a Member State in which he would otherwise be entitled to the benefit, this undoubtedly represents a threat to the standard of living of the Turkish people. The direct application of the export principle therefore contributes towards improving this standard of living.

As a matter of fact, this issue is currently discussed before the ECJ in case C-485/07 *Akdas and Others*. This case concerns Turkish workers who used to work in the Netherlands and have returned to Turkey. They receive a Dutch invalidity benefit which continues to be payable to them even when they reside in Turkey. However, as of 1 January 2003[31] a supplement to this invalidity benefit is no longer exported as a result of the changes in the Dutch legislation in this respect. Furthermore, this supplementary benefit is considered to be a special non-contributory benefit within the meaning of Regulation 1408/71, which, in the context of the Community co-ordination system is not exportable within the EU. The special non-contributory benefits mentioned in Annex IIa of this regulation are granted exclusively to persons who reside in the territory of the competent Member State (Article 10a of Regulation 1408/71). The relevant Dutch supplement was introduced in the list of Annex IIa in 2005.[32] In the context of the implementation of this special co-ordination regime the export of this supplement within the EU was phased out, starting in 2005 and stopping on 1 January 2007.

Yet, this special co-ordination system, which was not introduced until 1992 by Regulation (EEC) No 1247/92 of 30 April 1992[33] and which was subsequently

31 After a phasing out period which started in 2000.

32 See Regulation 647/2005, *OJ* L 117, 5.4.2005, 1.

33 *OJ* L 136, 19.5.1992.

amended in 2005, is not foreseen in Decision 3/80. The provision of Article 10a of Regulation 1408/71 was how the Council reacted in 1992 to the Court of Justice's case law, according to which these benefits had to be exported in accordance with the provisions of Article 10 of the Regulation.[34] Since Decision 3/80 has never been modified, by introducing a provision such as Article 10a of Regulation No 1408/71, this old case law could still apply for Turkish workers.

In order to find out whether this is the correct interpretation of Article 6 of Decision 3/80 a Dutch Court asked the ECJ for a preliminary ruling on questions regarding:

- the direct effect of Article 6 of Decision 3/80;
- the effect of amendments to Regulation 1408/71 since the adoption of Decision 3/80 on 19 September 1980, in particular the introduction of a special co-ordination regime for the non-contributory special benefits;
- the significance of Article 59 of the Additional Protocol; and
- the possibility to have different dates for the phasing out of the export of the benefit for export to Turkey compared to the dates for export within the EU.

As already mentioned above, there should be no problem for the ECJ, taking into account its previous case law on this matter, to recognise in principle the direct effect of the obligation in Article 6 to export the there mentioned benefits to Turkey. Moreover, since the limitations to the export of these benefits introduced in 1992 in Regulation 1408/71 were not taken over in Decision 3/80, the old case law of the ECJ would continue to apply, guaranteeing also the export of the non-contributory benefits to Turkey, where this is not guaranteed any more for export within the EU. Therefore the central question in this case seems to be whether this kind of favourable treatment for Turkish migrant workers compared to intra-EU migrant workers is compatible with Article 59 of the Additional Protocol which stipulates that "*in the fields covered by this Protocol Turkey shall not receive more favourable treatment than that which Member States grant to one another pursuant to the Treaty establishing the Community*".

The ECJ already stated in *Derin* (18 June 2007) that the rule laid down in Article 59 of the Additional Protocol would be infringed if a member of the family of a migrant Turkish worker who has been authorised to join that worker in a Member State would find himself in a more favourable situation than a family member of a national of a Member State.[35] As Advocate General Bot said in his opinion in

34 See *inter alia: Hughes*, paras 15 and 17; *Commission v Luxembourg (C-111/91)*, para 29 and *Acciardi*, para 14.

35 *Derin*, para 69.

this case, it can hardly be disputed that, although Article 59 refers only to the 'Republic of Turkey', it must be understood as laying down a limit to the scope of the rights that may be conferred on Turkish nationals by virtue of the Additional Protocol. It may therefore be concluded that, by virtue of Article 59 of the Additional Protocol, the rights conferred by Decision 3/80 on Turkish nationals cannot be more favourable than those enjoyed by nationals of the Member States and their family members on the basis of EC law on the freedom of movement of workers, by which the parties to the Association agreed to be guided.[36] In this line of reasoning, once export of a benefit is not guaranteed any more within the context of EU law on the free movement of workers, it should not be guaranteed any longer for Turkish workers who have returned to Turkey.

However, it remains to be seen whether the different dates for the phasing out of the export of the benefits applied for export to Turkey compared to export within the EU is in line with the non-discrimination principle of Decision 3/80 and Article 9 of the Association Agreement. Such a difference is likely to be seen as indirectly discriminatory on grounds of nationality as it probably affects Turkish workers more than workers of the Member States. Because of this the same phasing out period in national law should be applied for both export within the EU as for export to Turkey. Mr Akdas and the others should therefore be guaranteed export of the supplement to the Dutch invalidity benefits until 1 January 2007.

Of course we need to wait for the ECJ's ruling in this case to know the final answers to these questions.

3. THE AGREEMENTS WITH THE MAGHREB COUNTRIES

3.1. AGREEMENTS CONCLUDED IN 1976

On 25, 26 and 27 April 1976 the EEC signed three Cooperation Agreements with Tunisia, Algeria and Morocco (hereinafter also referred to as the "Maghreb countries"). These Agreements were approved on behalf of the EEC by three Council Regulations of 26 September 1978.[37]

---

36 Opinion of 11 January 2007, paras 102–104.

37 See Regulations (EEC) No 2210/78, 2211/78 and 2212/78 of 26 September 1978, *OJ* L 263/1, 264/1 and 265/1 of 27 September 1978. The text of the Agreements was also published in these *Official Journals*.

The objective of these Cooperation Agreements is to establish wide-ranging cooperation which will contribute to the economic and trade cooperation between these states and the EEC. They include provisions on the cooperation in the field of labour.[38]

First of all, these provisions confirm the prohibition of discrimination on grounds of nationality as regards working conditions or remuneration for workers of the Maghreb countries as well as for nationals of a Member State as far as the application of the law of the Maghreb states is concerned.

The Cooperation Agreements also include provisions in relation to the social security rights of workers of the contracting states and of the members of their family.[39] To start with, they guarantee workers holding the nationality of these states as well as any members of their families living with them, freedom from any discrimination based on nationality as far as social security is concerned. They further confirm the need to add together all periods of insurance, employment or residence completed by such workers in the various Member States for the purpose of pensions and annuities in respect of old age, invalidity and death and also for medical care for workers and for members of their families residing in the Community. They provide that workers in question shall receive family allowances for members of their families who are resident in the Community, excluding however residence in a Maghreb country. They also stipulate that the workers in question shall be able to transfer freely to the Maghreb countries, at the rates applied by virtue of the law of the debtor Member States, any pensions or annuities in respect of old age, death, industrial accident of occupational disease, or of invalidity resulting from industrial accident or occupational disease.

The ECJ considered that the purpose of the Cooperation Agreement is not to enable nationals of the Maghreb countries to move freely within the Community but to consolidate the position of Moroccan workers and members of their families living with them in the host Member State as regards social security.[40]

These Cooperation Agreements, comparably to the Association Agreement with Turkey, entrust the Cooperation Council with the task of adopting before the end of the first year following the entry into force of the Agreements, provisions to implement the *principles* set out in the relevant articles. It is remarkable that the word *principles* is used and not the word *rights and obligations*. However, no such

38 Articles 39–42 in the Agreement with Tunisia, Articles 38–41 in the Agreement with Algeria and Articles 40–43 in the Agreement with Morocco. These provisions are identical.

39 Respectively Article 40 (Tunisia), Article 39 (Algeria) and Article 41 (Morocco).

40 *Mesbah*, para 36 and *Fahmi*, para 56.

implementation measures were ever adopted or even proposed by the Commission.

Finally, these Cooperation Agreements confirm that the provisions adopted by the Cooperation Council shall not affect any rights or obligations arising from bilateral agreements linking the Maghreb countries and the Member States where those agreements provide for more favourable treatment of nationals of the contracting states. Clearly, as also follows from the analysis below, the social security co-ordination provided for in the context of these Cooperation Agreements, is only partial and needs to be complemented by bilateral agreements between the Member States and the Maghreb countries.

Furthermore, since the adoption of Regulation 859/2003 on the extension of the personal scope of Regulation 1408/71 to third-country nationals, the latter co-ordination instrument applies to nationals of the Maghreb countries legally residing on the territory of a Member State and as far as they are in a situation which is not confined in all respects within a single Member State. This implies the application to workers of the Maghreb countries and their family members of, for instance, the aggregation rules and the rules on export of benefits within the Member States of Regulation 1408/71.

3.2. ECJ'S CASE LAW ON THESE COOPERATION AGREEMENTS

3.2.1. *The Direct Effect and the Meaning of the Prohibition of Discrimination on Grounds of Nationality*

From the 90s onwards, the ECJ developed decisive case law with regard to the legal effect of the provisions on social security in these Agreements. In the first place the ECJ had to decide whether it was at all possible for these provisions to have a direct effect and to introduce legal obligations for the Member States *vis-à-vis* workers of the Maghreb countries and the members of their families.

The basis of this case law was the ECJ's crucial judgement of 31 January 1991 in *Kziber.* Building on its previous rulings on the direct applicability of provisions of international agreements concluded by the Community, in particular in the above-mentioned *Demirel,* the ECJ confirmed that the non-discrimination clauses of the Cooperation Agreements with the Maghreb countries also lay down in clear, precise and unconditional terms that in the field of social security discrimination, based on nationality, against workers holding the nationality of the Maghreb countries and the members of their families living with them is prohibited. It is therefore not subject, in its implementation or effects, to the adoption of any subsequent measure. The Court added that the object of the Cooperation Agreements to promote overall cooperation between the contracting parties, in particular in the field of labour, confirms that the principle of non-discrimination enshrined in the Agreements is capable of governing the legal situation of individuals.[41]

Despite the explicit request by Germany to the Court in the next case that was referred to it, namely *Yousfi*, to reconsider its findings on the direct effect of the non-discrimination clauses, in the Cooperation Agreements with the Maghreb countries, the ECJ has consistently confirmed its position on numerous occasions.[42]

The ECJ clarified that the principle of non-discrimination means that the persons covered by this provision must be treated as if they were nationals of the Member States concerned.[43] That principle therefore requires that persons falling within the scope of that provision of the Cooperation Agreement may claim social security benefits under the same conditions as nationals of the host Member State without it being possible for the legislation of that Member State to impose upon those persons more or stricter conditions than those applicable to its nationals.[44] Accordingly, the imposition on persons covered by the relevant provisions in the Cooperation Agreement not only of the requirement that they must be nationals of the Member State concerned but also of any other condition which is not required in respect of nationals must be regarded as incompatible with that principle of non-discrimination.[45]

It is worth mentioning that the ECJ recognised the added value of this principle over the extension of Regulation 1408/71 to third-country nationals by the above-mentioned Regulation 859/2003. In *El Youssfi* the ECJ said that third-country nationals who have no link with at least two Member States cannot make use of the non-discrimination clause of Article 3 Regulation 1408/71, but conversely may rely on the comparable provisions of the Cooperation Agreements when they have a link with only one Member State.[46]

---

41 *Kziber*, paras 15–21.

42 *Yousfi*, paras 16–19; *Hallouzi-Choho*, paras 19–20; *Krid*, paras 21–24; *Alami*, para 22; *Haddad*, para 26; *Babahenini*, paras 17 and 18 and, by analogy, *Echouikh*, para 39.

43 See, *inter alia*, *Hallouzi-Choho*, para 35; *Alami*, para 30 and *Echouikh*, para 55.

44 See, *inter alia*, *Hallouzi-Choho*, para 36; *Alami*, para 31; *Babahenini*, para 29 and *Echouikh* para 56.

45 See *Hallouzi-Choho*, para 37; *Alami*, para 32; *Babahenini*, para 30 and *Echouikh*, para 57.

46 *El Youssfi*, para 43–45.

3.2.2. *The Concept of Social Security Within the Meaning of the Cooperation Agreements*

Since *Kziber* the Court repeatedly held that the concept of social security in the Cooperation Agreements with the Maghreb countries must be deemed to bear the same meaning as the identical concept used in Regulation 1408/71.[47] Particularly with regard to the so-called special non-contributory benefits, the ECJ has confirmed that these benefits fell within the matters covered by Regulation 1408/71 by virtue of Article 4(1) thereof and therefore also under the scope of the relevant provisions of the Cooperation Agreements.[48]

Accordingly the ECJ applied the non-discrimination clause of these Agreements to a wide range of social security benefits, such as:

- tideover allowance for young jobseekers (*Kziber*);
- disability allowance (*Yousfi*, *Mesbah* and *Babahenini*);
- transitional benefits for the Dutch general old-age insurance scheme (*Hallouzi-Choho*);
- unemployment benefit (*Alami*);
- supplementary allowance paid by the national solidarity fund (*Krid*).

3.2.3. *The Concept of Workers and of Members of the Family*

In contrast to the concept of social security for which the Court refers to the meaning of this concept in Regulation 1408/71, the ECJ adopted another line of reasoning in respect of the concepts of "worker" and of "member of the family" in the Cooperation Agreements.

Regarding the concept of workers, Regulation 1408/71, in its Article 1, develops very complex definitions in order to determine who is to be considered as an employed person for the purpose of the application of this Regulation. These definitions basically refer to definitions established by the national legislation of the Member States. With regard to the concept of worker under the non-discrimination clauses of the Cooperation Agreements, the ECJ seems to accord this concept an autonomous meaning. The Court does not refer to any definition in national law but merely states that it encompasses active workers as well as those who have left the labour market, either after reaching the age required for receipt of an old-age pension or after becoming the victims of one of the risks

---

47 *Kziber*, para 25; *Yousfi*, para 24; *Hallouzi-Choho*, para 25; *Alami*, para 23; *Haddad*, para 27; *Krid*, para 32; *Babahenini*, para 26 and *Echouikh*, para 51.

48 See *inter alia Krid*, para 32–33.

creating entitlement to allowances falling under other branches of social security.[49] This case law makes no reference to definitions of worker in the national legislation of Member States.

Furthermore, the ECJ seems to have adopted the same position with regard to the concept of "member of the family". Under Regulation 1408/71 this concept is defined in Article 1(f) as meaning any person defined or recognised as a member of the family or designated as a member of the household by the legislation under which benefits are provided (with special definitions for the implementation of the provisions on sickness benefits or benefits for disabled persons). Yet, according to the ECJ's case law on the Cooperation Agreements with the Maghreb countries, the concept of "member of the family" once again seems to have an autonomous meaning independent of any definition or recognition as such by the legislation of the Member States concerned. So the Court has declared that the term "members of the family" in these Agreements refers not only to the worker's spouse and descendants but also to persons having a close family relationship with him, such as his relatives in the ascending line, including those related to him by marriage.[50] It also covers family members of a migrant worker from a Maghreb country who, after the worker's death, continue to live in the Member State in which he was employed. So, for instance, this concept relates to a migrant worker's widow who lives in the Member State in which the worker spent all his working life before he died and who is the recipient there of a survivor's pension paid in consequence of that employment.[51] Unlike the definition in Regulation 1408/71, these definitions do not make any reference to the definitions used in the domestic legislation of the Member States involved.

Nonetheless, it follows from *Haddad* that the persons concerned must be family members of a "worker". In this judgement the ECJ stated that the concept of member of the family does not cover a student of Moroccan nationality, who is the unemployed wife of a non-active Moroccan national. The Court argued that even when the couple is residing in a Member State and insured on a voluntary basis under the sickness insurance scheme of that State, the wife is not covered as member of the family by these provisions of the Association Agreements, when it is not proven that she lives with a worker of Moroccan nationality with whom she has a close family relationship.[52] Again in this judgement the ECJ seems to indicate

---

49 See *inter alia Kziber*, para 27; *Alami*, para 27; and by analogy *El Yousffi*, para 65 en *Echouikh*, para 44. The latter judgement also confirmed that a person who fulfils compulsory or enlisted military service is to be considered as a 'worker' (para 47).

50 *Mesbah*, para 46 and by analogy, *El Yousffi* para 68.

51 *Krid, para* 30–31.

52 Order of 27 April 2004 in *Haddad*.

that close family relationship with a worker is sufficient to fall under the scope of the Agreements as member of the family of a worker.

With regard to family benefits the ECJ confirmed that the prohibition of discrimination laid down in Article 41(1) of the Cooperation Agreement with Morocco is guaranteed only within the limits of the conditions laid down in Article 41(3) meaning that, unless the children of a Moroccan worker reside in the Community, neither that worker nor his children can rely on the principle of the prohibition of discrimination. Export to Morocco of family benefits is not guaranteed by the non-discrimination clause.[53]

With regard to one aspect of the rights of family members of workers, the ECJ's case law turned out to be quite controversial in the 90s. In *Kziber* the Court applied the non-discrimination clause to a benefit (the Belgian tideover allowance for young jobseekers who had just left school) which was a benefit they were entitled to in their own right and not a derived right as member of the family of a worker. Previously the ECJ had refused to apply the provisions of Regulation 1408/71 to family members claiming such a personal right. In its judgement in *Kermashek*, delivered in 1976, the Court decided that Regulation 1408/71 applies to two distinct categories: workers on the one hand, members of their family on the other. Whereas the persons belonging to the first category may claim the rights to benefits envisaged by Regulation 1408/71 as rights of their own, members of the family can only claim derived rights, that is to say rights acquired through their status as a member of the family of a worker. From this it was concluded that the members of the family of migrant workers are entitled only to the benefits provided by the national legislation of the Member States for the members of the family, as such, of migrant workers.[54] On the Belgian tideover allowance for young jobseekers, the Court, in its judgement in *Deak*, had taken the view that this allowance constituted a benefit available to young persons in search of employment by reason of their personal situation and not by virtue of their status as members of the family of a worker. The right was a personal one which the members of the family of a migrant worker may not, as a result, claim on the basis of Regulation 1408/71.

In *Kziber* however, contrary to what the AG and the intervening Member States had submitted on the basis of the previous case law in *Kermashek* and *Deak*, the ECJ ruled, without further explanation, that as regards the scope of the rights of a member of the family of a Moroccan worker, living with him, the principle of freedom from all discrimination, based on nationality, means that such a person,

53 *Fahmi*, para 56–57.
54 *Kermachek*, paras 7–9.

who satisfies all the conditions laid down by national legislation for the purpose of entitlement to the relevant benefits, may not be refused those benefits on ground of his nationality.[55] In its judgement the ECJ made no reference at all to the distinction between personal rights and derived rights.

As a result Community workers' families would receive treatment less favourable than that accorded to families of workers who were nationals of a non-member country with which the Community had concluded these Cooperation Agreements. The application of the distinction between personal rights and derived rights only to members of the families of Community workers and not also to members of the families of workers who are nationals of States with which the Community has concluded such Agreements was considered as giving rise to discrimination.

As a matter of fact, and this has been recognised explicitly by the Court in *Krid*, the persons covered by the non-discrimination clause of the Cooperation Agreements are not the same as those covered by the personal scope of Regulation 1408/71 (as defined by its Article 2), since the case law distinguishing between the derived rights and the personal rights of members of migrant workers' families in the context of Regulation 1408/71 cannot be applied in the context of the Cooperation Agreements.[56] A person comes within the scope *ratione personae* of the non-discrimination clause of the Cooperation Agreements, irrespective of whether the benefit for which he/she has applied is awarded to a recipient as a personal right or in that person's capacity as a member of the family of a Maghreb migrant worker.

The clear contradiction between the case law on Regulation 1408/71 on the one hand and the case law on the Cooperation Agreements on the other, with regard to personal rights of members of the family of migrant workers, was later tempered by the judgement in *Cabanis-Issarte*.[57] In this judgement the Court stated that Article 3(1) of Regulation 1408/71 grants the right to equal treatment as regards application of the social security legislation of the Member States, without drawing any distinction between workers, members of workers' families or their surviving spouses. In the same judgement, the Court also stated that the distinction between rights in person and derived rights may undermine the fundamental Community law requirement that its rules should be applied uniformly, by making their

55 *Kziber*, para 28.

56 *Krid*, paras 38–39, on the claim, by the widow of an Algerian worker, of the French supplementary allowance from the FNS, being a personal right and not a derived right acquired through the claimant' s status as a member of the family of a migrant worker. See also *Hallouzi-Choho*, para 30 en *Babahenni*, paras 24–25.

57 *Cabanis-Issarte*, paras 30–31.

applicability to individuals depend on whether the national law relating to the benefits in question treats the rights concerned as rights in person or as derived rights, in the light of specific features of the domestic social security scheme.

Consequently, even if the ECJ continues to confirm that the scope *ratione personae* of Regulation 1408/71 and of the Cooperation Agreements as far as members of the family are concerned are not the same[58], the implementation of the non-discrimination clauses in these instruments seems to be streamlined now.

3.2.4. Persons with Dual Nationality: The Mesbah Judgement

On another point the ECJ's case law on the Cooperation Agreements remains also very controversial. The consequences of this case law may even affect the implementation of various instruments of secondary Community legislation applicable to third-country nationals that were adopted since the introduction of Title IV in the EC Treaty. It concerns persons holding dual nationality: the nationality of one of the Maghreb countries, or of a third country in general, and the nationality of the host Member State.

The *Mesbah* case concerned the mother-in-law of a Moroccan migrant worker who had acquired the nationality of his host Member State (Belgium) without losing his Moroccan nationality. This occurred before the date on which the family member concerned began to live with him there and applied for a social security benefit under the law of that State. The question arose if this member of the family may, in reliance on the non-discrimination clauses in the Cooperation Agreements, invoke that worker's Moroccan nationality as a basis for claiming the benefit on the principle of equal treatment in the field of social security.

In this case both the Commission and the Advocate General submitted that, if a worker has the nationality of both his country of origin and his host Member State, it follows by analogy with the *Micheletti* judgement that Community law precludes the host State from preventing his family member from invoking the worker's (Moroccan) nationality to obtain the benefit on the principle of equal treatment in the field of social security, solely on the ground that, under the law of the host State, the worker is regarded as a national of that Member State alone.[59]

As regards Community law on the free movement of EU-citizens, the ECJ indeed consistently held that it is not permissible for a Member State to restrict the effects of the grant of the nationality of another Member State by imposing an additional

58 See most recently *El Youssfi*, para 62.

59 *Mesbah*, para 28. See also paras 46–52 of the opinion of AG Alber in this case.

condition for recognition of that nationality with a view to the exercise of the fundamental freedoms provided for in the Treaty.[60] Thus, the Court held that once the person concerned has established his status as a national of a Member State, the other Member States are not entitled to challenge that status on the ground that the person concerned might also have the nationality of a non-member country which, under the legislation of the host Member State, overrides that of the Member State.

In *Mesbah*, however, the ECJ stated that Community law allows a host Member State to prevent a member of the family of a worker of Belgian nationality from relying on that worker's Moroccan nationality in order to obtain the benefit of the principle of equal treatment in the field of social security. The Belgian government had indicated that under its legislation the worker is considered to be a national of that State alone. In the ECJ's view it is for the national court alone, to determine the nationality of Mrs Mesbah's son-in-law in accordance with the Belgian law, applicable at the time when the application for disability allowance was made and during the relevant reference periods for assessing entitlement to that social security benefit. For the Court a Moroccan migrant worker, when that worker also has the nationality of the host Member State, could invoke his Moroccan nationality, for the purposes of the application of Article 41(1) of the Agreement, solely on the basis of the law of the Member State concerned, which it is for the national court alone, however, to interpret and apply in the proceedings before it.[61]

This position was more recently confirmed by the Court in *El Youssfi* (17 April 2007) on the non-discrimination clause in the new Association Agreement with Morocco (see below). The ECJ stated again that it is for the national court to ascertain, on the basis of the legislation of the host Member State, if a member of the family of a Moroccan migrant worker who is also a national of that State may, under its legislation, rely on the worker's Moroccan nationality for the purposes of the application of the first subparagraph of Article 65(1) of the Association Agreement.[62]

Almost 10 years later, this ruling continues to surprise. The Court let it depend on the national legislation of the host Member State of which the national of a Maghreb state holds the nationality, to determine whether this worker may also rely on his nationality of a Maghreb country. The most crucial factor is that in doing so the Court makes it acceptable, under the Cooperation Agreements, for national law to deny a member of the family of a worker holding the nationality

60 See, in particular, *Micheletti*, para 10 and *Garcia Avello*, para 28.
61 *Mesbah*, paras 39–41.
62 *Mesbah*, para 72.

of one of the Contracting States, the right to rely on this nationality. Consequently, it is permissible that a Member State's own nationality is given precedence over that of a third country with the result that the person concerned is denied a certain right. In this case the effects of a worker's Moroccan nationality is restricted with a view to the exercise of the rights vested in him (and the members of his family) as a Moroccan by the Cooperation Agreement. As far as he himself is concerned, no such restriction is initially apparent since he is not subject to discrimination if his, in this case Belgian, nationality is recognised and he may rely on it. However, the exercise of rights of the members of his family might be restricted if they are denied the right to rely on the Agreement

One could submit that if reliance on Moroccan nationality were also possible, the person possessing both nationalities would be granted greater rights than other citizens of the European Union. In this case for example, the Moroccan mother-in-law of a Belgian worker could have no right to certain benefits, whereas the Moroccan mother-in-law of a Moroccan worker has such a right on account of the principle of non-discrimination contained in the Cooperation Agreement. However, this is a consequence of the Cooperation Agreements themselves and the rights established therein. It is not due to the fact that the worker invokes both nationalities.[63]

Finally, it does not seem to be consistent with the obligations taken by the Community *vis-à-vis* the Maghreb countries, not to recognise, for the purpose of the implementation of these Cooperation Agreements, the nationality these states grant to persons. Indeed, no provisions whatsoever in these Agreements limit the consequences of the grant of nationality by these states to persons.

Furthermore, this case law of the ECJ could have wide-ranging consequences for the implementation of various recently adopted Community legal instruments which are applicable to third-country nationals. This is for instance the case with Directive 2003/86 on the right to family reunification.[64] If Member States could exclude from the scope of these EC legal instruments persons holding the nationality of a third country, but who acquired the nationality of the host Member States while maintaining the nationality of the third country, acquiring the nationality of the host Member States could lead to a loss of rights. This is more specifically the case where the rights guaranteed under these Community instruments are possibly broader than the rights guaranteed under the national

63 See also the opinion of AG Alber in this case, paras 44–51.

64 Directive 2003/86 of the Council of 22 September 2003 on the right to family reunification, *OJ* L 251, 3.10.2003, 12.

law of that Member State alone, which indeed might be the case with the family reunification directive.

3.3. THE EURO-MEDITERRANEAN ASSOCIATION AGREEMENTS SIGNED IN 1995, 1996 AND 2002

3.3.1. Their Meaning and Provisions on Social Security

Meanwhile the above analysed Cooperation Agreements with the Maghreb countries have been replaced by a set of new agreements with these countries, called Euro-Mediterranean Agreements and establishing an Association between the EC and its Member States and the Maghreb countries (hereinafter referred to as the 'Association Agreements'). These are:

- the Agreement with Tunisia signed on 17 July 1995 and approved on behalf of the Communities by Decision of 26 January 1998[65];
- the Agreement with Morocco signed on 26 February 1996 and approved on behalf of the Communities by Decision of 24 January 2000[66]; and
- the Agreement with Algeria signed on 22 April 2002 and approved on behalf of the Communities by Decision of 18 July 2005.[67]

The aims of these Agreements are, amongst others, to provide an appropriate framework for political dialogue between the Parties, [...] to promote [...] the expansion of harmonious economic and social relations between the Parties and to promote economic, social, cultural and financial cooperation (Article 1). As regards social matters, they include some provisions on workers and their social security rights comparable to the ones in the Cooperation Agreements of the 70s.[68]

There are however some interesting differences. Articles 65 (Tunisia and Morocco) and 68 (Algeria) confirm, for the workers of these states and any members of their family living with them, the principle of non-discrimination on grounds of nationality in the Member States in which they are employed. In contrast to the provisions in the Cooperation Agreements these provisions define the term 'social security'. It covers the branches of social security dealing with sickness and maternity benefits, invalidity, old-age and survivors' benefits, industrial accident

65 *OJ* L 97, 30.3.1998, 1.

66 *OJ* L 70, 18.3.2000, 1.

67 *OJ* L 265, 10.10.2005, 1.

68 See Articles 65–68 of the Agreement with Tunisia and of the Agreement with Morocco and articles 68–71 of the Agreement with Algeria.

and occupational disease benefits and death, unemployment and family benefits. Since these branches are the same as the ones covered by Regulation 1408/71, this provision does not really add any value to what the ECJ had already decided in the above mentioned case law, i.e. that the material scope of the Cooperation Agreements was identical to the scope of Regulation 1408/71. Moreover, and newly, they stipulate that these provisions shall not, however, cause the other co-ordination rules provided for in Community legislation based on Article 42 EC to apply, except if so provided for by the Association Council. This provision means that the internal Community co-ordination in Regulation 1408/71 cannot be considered to be automatically applicable to workers of the Maghreb countries. In this respect we should remember that these Association Agreements were signed before the adoption of Regulation 859/2003 extending the scope of Regulation 1408/71 to third-country nationals.

The provisions on social security rights further confirm the need to add together all periods of insurance, employment or residence completed by such workers in the various Member States for the purpose of pensions and annuities in respect of old age, invalidity and survivors' pension and family, sickness and maternity benefits (the latter three were not mentioned in the Cooperation Agreements) and also for medical care for workers and for members of their families residing in the Community. They stipulate that the workers in question shall receive family allowances for members of their families who are resident in the Community and that the workers in question shall be able to transfer freely to the Maghreb countries, at the rates applied by virtue of the law of the debtor Member States, any pensions or annuities in respect of old age, death, industrial accident of occupational disease, or of invalidity resulting from an industrial accident or occupational disease. However, this time special non-contributory benefits are excluded from the free transfer to the Maghreb countries.

Remarkably, the Association Agreements specify that the provisions in the Chapter on workers shall not apply to nationals of the Parties residing or working illegally in the territory of their host countries.[69] Comparable provisions were not included in the Cooperation Agreements. It remains unclear what exactly is meant with "illegally". However, the exclusion not only refers to illegal residence but also to illegal employment, including of those legally resident. It remains to be seen what could be the consequences of this exclusion for the social security rights of these persons.[70]

---

69 See Article 66 of the Agreement with Tunisia and of the Agreement with Morocco and Article 69 of the Agreement with Algeria.

70 On the social security rights of persons illegally resident or working in the host state: see the contribution of Klaus Kapuy.

The Agreements also entrust the Association Council with the task of adopting, before the end of the first year following the entry into force of the Agreements, provisions to implement the *principles* set out in the relevant articles. Again the word *principles* is used and not the words *rights and obligations.*[71]

Finally, they confirm that the provisions adopted by the Association Council shall not affect any rights or obligations arising from bilateral agreements linking the Maghreb countries and the Member States where those agreements provide for more favourable treatment of nationals of the contracting states.[72]

Furthermore, joint declarations relating to Article 65 are attached to the Agreements with Tunisia and with Morocco, saying that it is understood that the term 'members of their family' shall be defined according to the national legislation of the host country concerned.

3.3.2. The ECJ's Case Law on the Association Agreements with the Maghreb Countries

The ECJ already had the opportunity to shed light on the meaning of the provisions on social security in these Association Agreements. In *Echouikh* the Court confirmed that their non-discrimination clauses are formulated in terms identical to those of the Cooperation Agreements so that its case law on the latter is fully transposable to the first. This conclusion does not only concern the direct effect of these clauses but also their meaning. The ECJ underlined that the aims of the Association Agreements may be viewed as directly furthering those on which the Cooperation Agreements are based.[73] The Court drew the same conclusion on the concept of worker, which encompasses both active workers and those who have left the labour market after reaching the age required for receipt of an old-age pension or after becoming the victims of one of the risks creating entitlement to allowances falling under other branches of social security and including also civil servants.[74]

For the Court this is also true for the concept of social security, which is deemed to bear the same meaning as the identical term used in Council Regulation 1408/71.[75] This means that the definition of social security introduced in the

71 See Articles 67 of the Agreement with Tunisia and of the Agreement with Morocco and Article 70 of the Agreement with Algeria.
72 See Articles 68 of the Agreement with Tunisia and of the Agreement with Morocco and Article 71 of the Agreement with Algeria.
73 *Echouikh*, paras 40–42 and 55–58; *El Youssfi*, paras 51–53.
74 *Echouikh*, paras 44 and 47; *El Youssfi*, para 65.
75 *Echouikh*, paras 50–51 (on an armed services invalidity pension). See also *El Youssfi* para 57 (on the Belgian Guaranteed Income for Elderly Persons).

relevant articles of the Association Agreements do not alter their material scope compared to this of the Cooperation Agreements.

As already mentioned before, joint declarations are attached to the Agreements with Tunisia and with Morocco, saying that it is understood that the term 'members of their family' shall be defined according to the national legislation of the host country concerned. Despite these declarations, the ECJ repeated in *El Youssfi* its above analysed case law on the Cooperation Agreements. The Court confirmed that the scope *ratione personae* of the first subparagraph of Article 65(1) of the Euro-Mediterranean Agreement with Morocco is not the same as that of Article 2 of Regulation 1408/71 with the result that the case law in which a distinction is drawn between the derived rights and the personal rights of the members of the migrant worker's family in the context of that regulation – as clarified by the judgment in *Cabanis-Issarte* – cannot be applied in the context of the Association Agreements. The Court repeated furthermore that the term 'members of the family' refers not only to the worker's spouse and descendants but also to persons having a close family relationship with him such as his relatives in the ascending line, including those related to him by marriage. The ECJ hereby confirmed the autonomous meaning of the concept of 'member of the family', i.e. not dependent on any definition under the national legislation of the host country.[76] Apparently the ECJ does not seem to attach any value to the joint declarations as regards the concept of 'members of the family', annexed to the Association Agreements.

3.3.3. *The Commission's Proposals of December 2007 to Implement these Agreements*

On 11 and 12 December 2007 the Commission adopted proposals for a Council decision on the position to be taken by the Community within the relevant Association Councils with regard to the adoption of provisions on the co-ordination of the social security systems.[77] These almost identical proposals are part of a package which includes similar proposals with regard to the Association Agreements with Croatia, the former Yugoslav Republic of Macedonia and Israel.[78]

The Commission submitted a proposal to the EC Council of Ministers to agree on draft decisions of the Association Councils. This draft should be the basis for the

---

76 *El Youssfi*, paras 62 and 68.

77 COM(2007) 788 (Tunisia); COM(2007) 790 (Algeria) and COM(2007) 792 (Morocco).

78 COM(2007) 787 (the former Yugoslav Republic of Macedonia); COM(2007) 789 (Croatia) and COM(2007) 793 (Israel).

Community's position within the Association Councils during the negotiations with the associated countries.

The proposed decisions provide for implementing measures with regard to those provisions of the Association Agreements in relation to social security which are not already covered by Regulation 859/2003 extending Regulation 1408/71 to third-country nationals, or declared by the Court to be directly applicable, such as the non-discrimination clauses. However, as Regulation 859/2003 is based on Title IV of the EC Treaty, in accordance with Articles 1 and 2 of the Protocol on the position of Denmark annexed to the EC Treaty, Denmark is not bound by or subject to it. Therefore the Commission proposed an article (Article 6) clarifying that Denmark shall use, in favour of workers of the Maghreb countries, the relevant provisions of Regulations 1408/71 and 574/72 in order to implement the principles of aggregation and of export of benefits foreseen in the Association Agreements.

The proposed Article 1 defines the terms "Agreement", "Regulation", "implementing Regulation", "Member State", "worker", "member of the family", "legislation", "benefits" and "family benefits", and refers to Regulations 1408/71 and 574/72 for the other terms used in the proposed decisions. Remarkably, for the terms "worker" and "members of the family" the draft decisions refer to their definitions used in Regulation 1408/71 for the purpose of the legislation of a Member State and to the legislation of the Maghreb countries for the purpose of that legislation. These proposals seem to depart from the above analysed case law of the ECJ, including that on the Association Agreements, giving autonomous meaning to the concepts of workers and of members of the family.

In line with the wording of the Association Agreements, the proposed Article 2 defines the personal scope of the decisions as relating to workers legally employed in the host country (legal residence does not seem to be required) and the members of their family legally resident with the worker in that country.

Part II covers the relations between the Member States and the Maghreb countries. Article 4 contains the principle of the export of cash benefits (waiving of residence clauses) as provided for by the Association Agreements.[79] The proposed Article 4 shows that this principle is limited to the benefits within the meaning of Article 1(h) of the proposed Decisions, being old-age or survivors pensions, benefits in respect of accidents at work and occupational diseases or of invalidity benefits resulting from accidents at work and occupational diseases. Special non-

79 See Articles 65(4) of the Agreement with Tunisia and of the Agreement with Morocco and Article 68(4) of the Agreement with Algeria.

contributory cash benefits as set out in Annex IIa of Regulation 1408/71 are excluded as well as corresponding benefits from the Maghreb countries as set out in the Annexes of the decisions.

Article 5 specifies which persons covered by this proposal are entitled to family benefits on behalf of the competent state. The proposed Decisions ensure that the provisions on the export of benefits and the granting of family benefits apply to EU workers legally employed in the Maghreb countries and to their family members legally resident there.

However, no provision is proposed for family benefits to be received by legally employed Maghreb workers in the EU, nor for their members of family legally resident in the EU. A provision stipulating that the workers in question shall receive family allowances for members of their families who are resident in the Community is already present in the Association Agreements.[80, 81] The Commission was clearly, and quite rightly, of the opinion that the provisions in this regard in the Association Agreements are having direct effect and that no further implementation measures are necessary for these categories of workers and the members of their families. However, taking into account the most recent case law of the ECJ it should be noted that the concepts of "worker" and of "family members" under the Association Agreements seem to have an autonomous meaning, where these concepts under the proposed decisions of the Association Councils are defined by referring to the legislation of the relevant Member States.

It is also unclear whether there is a difference in meaning between the concept of "family allowances" in the Association Agreements and "family benefits" in the proposed decisions. In the latter, reference is made to the definition of family benefits in Article 1(u)(i) of Regulation 1408/71, which refers to "*all benefits in kind or in cash intended to meet family expenses*". This article of Regulation 1408/71 also provides for a definition of "family allowances" being "*periodical cash benefits granted exclusively by reference to the number and, where appropriate, the age of members of the family*". The latter definition evidently covers fewer categories of benefits compared to the definition of family benefits, which includes for instance all kinds of parental benefits. Does this mean that the relevant provisions in the Association Agreements, for which the Commission did not

80 See Articles 65(3) of the Agreement with Tunisia and of the Agreement with Morocco and Article 68(3) of the Agreement with Algeria.

81 Conversely, in the above mentioned proposed decisions of the Association Councils of the former Yugoslav Republic of Macedonia, Croatia and Israel, such provisions on workers and their family members in the EU are proposed, because no corresponding provisions are foreseen in the Agreements with these countries.

propose any implementing measure, have a smaller material scope than the corresponding provisions in the proposed decision for EU workers and the members of their families legally residing with these workers in a Maghreb country? Yet, there are clear contradictions with regard to this particular point in the different language versions of the Association Agreements. In the French and Dutch version of Articles 65(3) and 68(3) the concept of "prestations familiales" and of "gezinsbijslagen" is used, which correspond to the English "family benefits" in Article 1(u)(i) of Regulation 1408/71, whereas in the German version, the word "Familienbeihilfe" is used, corresponding to the notion of "family allowances" under Article 1(u)(ii) of Regulation 1408/71. In order to clarify this, it would be better to include a provision in the implementing decision on the right to family benefits for members of the family of Maghreb workers, residing in the EU.

As regards family benefits, we should finally underline that it clearly follows from these provisions that there is no entitlement to family benefits for family members of a Maghreb worker, if these family members reside outside the territory of the European Union.

Since the rules on aggregation of periods fulfilled under the legislation of the Member States is already guaranteed for third-country nationals legally residing in the Member States by Regulation 859/2003, it was not necessary to include such rules in the draft decision.

Furthermore, the Commission proposes some miscellaneous provisions with regard to administrative cooperation, checks and medical examinations as well as with regard to transitional provisions similar to those contained in Regulation 1408/71. Article 10 of the proposed Decisions specifies that provisions of bilateral agreements providing for more favourable treatment remain in force, as provided for in the Association Agreements.

These draft decisions only introduce rules on the external co-ordination between the social security schemes of the Member States on the one hand and those of the Maghreb countries on the other, based on the mandate given in the Association Agreements. However, this mandate and the proposed co-ordination only allow for a limited co-ordination, leaving important matters such as the determination of the applicable legislation, to the bilateral agreements concluded between these states.

4. CONCLUDING OBSERVATIONS

Over the last decades, the provisions on social security in the agreements concluded between Turkey and the Maghreb countries on one side and the EU on the other, have been playing a quite remarkable role in the legal position of these countries' migrant workers and their family members. Their implementation has been quite controversial and given rise to interesting case law of the European Court of Justice. However, their impact remains rather limited, except for the principle of non-discrimination on grounds of nationality whose direct effect was recognised by the ECJ and is therefore capable of governing the legal situation of individuals. The provisions on the right to family benefits for members of the family residing in the EU seem to have direct effect as well. It is not unlikely that the Court should come to the same conclusion with regard to the export principle, notably under Decision 3/80 (Turkey) in the *Akdas* case.

Taking into account the ECJ's case law on the lack of direct effect of other provisions, further developments of the external co-ordination between the social security schemes of the Member States and those of Turkey and the Maghreb countries, remain subject to the adoption of implementation measures by the relevant Association Councils. Negotiations on the implementation of Decision 3/80 have clearly been blocked ever since the 1980s and so far no new initiative has been taken by the Commission. For the Maghreb countries proposals of the Commission are on the table now. But even if such implementation measures were adopted under the mandate of the Agreements, there still will be large loopholes, such as the non-coverage of self-employed persons and of economically non-active persons like students. Neither have any provisions been adopted or even proposed, regarding rules to determine the applicable legislation in cross-border situations between Turkey and the Maghreb countries on the one side and the Member States on the other. As a result important scope has been left open to be filled in by bilateral agreements already concluded or still to be concluded between these countries and the individual Member States, in particular with regard to rules on the determination of applicable legislation. Moreover, since rules of this kind decide whether or not nationals of these countries are subject to the social security legislation of a Member State, they even hold the key for the application of the proposed external co-ordination measures, the latter's scope indeed being dependent on the workers involved being subject to the legislation of one or more Member Sates. This might, for instance, be problematic for posted workers or seasonal workers.

The limited importance of these instruments also follows from the adoption in 2003 at EC level of Regulation 859/2003, extending the scope of Regulation

1408/71 to third-country nationals legally residing on the territory of a Member State and in a situation which is not confined in all respects within a single Member State. This instrument renders superfluous the agreement on further measures for internal co-ordination of social security schemes of the Member States for citizens of Turkey and of the Maghreb countries. Therefore, Regulation 859/2003 already fulfils to a large extent the mandate in the Agreements with these countries, making further implementation by the Association Councils unnecessary for such internal co-ordination. However, since Regulation 859/2003 is not applicable to purely internal situations, the equal treatment provisions of which the ECJ recognised their direct effect, remains fully relevant for such situations. Neither does Regulation 859/2003 extend the provisions of Regulation 1408/71 to third-county nationals working on the territory of Member State(s) but not residing there. This might for instance be the case for workers and self-employed persons posted from Turkey and the Maghreb countries to the EU or even within the EU (such as transport workers) as well as for seasonal workers, of course as far as they are not considered as being resident in a Member State within the meaning of Regulation 859/2003. And finally, Regulation 859/2003 does not apply to Denmark. So, even if it is an enormous credit of this regulation to solve most of the internal EC co-ordination problems for nationals of Turkey and the Maghreb countries, it certainly does not solve all of them.

Therefore we might conclude that there is still a lot of work to be done, not only with a view to furthering the implementation of the Agreements, but also so as to adapt these Agreements to current and new forms of mobility between Turkey and the Maghreb countries on the one side and the EU Member States on the other.

ANNEX: LIST OF JUDGEMENTS OF THE ECJ REFERRED TO

Abatay: ECJ 21 October 2003, *Eran Abatay and Others and Nadi Sahin v Bundesanstalt für Arbeit,* Cases C-317/01 and C-369/01 [2003] ECR I-12301

Acciardi: ECJ 2 August 1993, *Genaro Acciardi v Commissie Beroepszaken Administratieve Geschillen in de Provincie Noord-Holland,* Case C-66/92 [1993] ECR I-4567

Alami: ECJ 12 February 2003, *Office national de l'emploi v Mohamed Alami,* Case C-23/02 [2003] ECR I-1399

Babahenini: ECJ 15 January 1998, *Henia Babahenini v Belgian State,* Case C-113/97 [1998] ECR I-183

Cabanis-Issarte: ECJ 30 April 1996, *Bestuur van de Sociale Verzekeringsbank v J.M. Cabanis-Issarte*, Case C-308/93 [1996] ECR I-2097

Commission v Luxembourg (C-111/91): ECJ 10 March 1993, *Commission of the European Communities v Grand Duchy of Luxembourg*, Case C-111/91 [1993] ECR I-817

Deak: ECJ 20 June 1985, *Office national de l'emploi v Joszef Deak*, Case 94/84 [1985] ECR 1873

Demirel: ECJ 30 September 1987, *Meryem Demirel v Stadt Schwäbisch Gmünd*, Case 12/86 [1987] ECR 3719

Derin: ECJ 18 July 2007, *Ismail Derin v Landkreis Darmstadt-Dieburg*, Case C-325/05 [2007] ECR I-6495

Echouikh: ECJ 13 June 2006, *Ameur Echouikh v Secrétaire d'État aux Anciens Combattants*, Case C-336/05 [2006] ECR I-5223

El Youssfi: ECJ 17 April 2007, *Mamate El Youssfi v Office national des pensions (ONP)*, Case C-276/06 [2007] ECR I-2851

Fahmi: ECJ 20 March 2001, *Hassan Fahmi and M. Esmoris Cerdeiro-Pinedo Amado v Bestuur van de Sociale Verzekeringsbank*, Case C-33/99 [2001] ECR I-2415

Garcia Avello: ECJ 2 October 2003, *Carlos Garcia Avello v Belgian State*, Case C-148/02 [2003] ECR I-11613

Günaydin: ECJ 30 September 1997, *Faik Günaydin, Hatice Günaydin, Günes Günaydin and Seda Günaydin v Freistaat Bayern*, Case C-36/96 [1997] ECR I-5143

Haddad: ECJ 27 April 2004, *Yamina Haddad v Belgian State*, Case C-358/02, *OJ* C 118, 30.4.2004, 26

Hallouzi-Choho: ECJ 3 October 1996, *A. Hallouzi-Choho v Bestuur van de Sociale Verzekeringsbank*, Case C-126/95 [1996] ECR I-4807

Hughes: ECJ 16 July 1992, *Rose Hughes v Chief Adjudication Officer, Belfast*, Case C-78/91 [1992] ECR I-4839

Kermaschek: ECJ 23 November 1976, *Slavica Kermaschek v Bundesanstalt für Arbeit*, Case 40/76 [1976] ECR 1669

Kocak and Örs: ECJ 14 March 2000, *Ibrahim Kocak v Landesversicherungsanstalt Oberfranken und Mittelfranken and Ramazan Örs v Bundesknappschaft*, Case C-102/98 and Case C-211/98 [2000] ECR I-1287

Krid: ECJ 5 April 1995, *Zoulika Krid v Caisse nationale d'assurance vieillesse des travailleurs salariés (CNAVTS)*, Case C-103/94 [1995] ECR I-719

Kus: ECJ 16 December 1992, *Kazim Kus v Landeshauptstadt Wiesbaden*, Case C-237/91 [1992] ECR I-6781

Kziber: ECJ 31 January 1991, *Kazim Kus v Landeshauptstadt Wiesbaden*, Case C-18/90 [1991] ECR I-199

Mesbah: ECJ 11 November 1999, *Belgian State v Fatna Mesbah*, Case C-179/98 [1999] ECR I-7955

Micheletti: ECJ 7 July 1992, *Mario Vicente Micheletti and others v Delegación del Gobierno en Cantabria*, Case C-369/90 [1992] ECR I-4239

Öztürk: ECJ 28 April 2004, *Sakir Öztürk v Pensionsversicherungsanstalt der Arbeiter*, Case C-373/02 [2004] ECR I-3605

Savas: ECJ 11 May 2000, *The Queen v Secretary of State for the Home Department, ex parte Abdulnasir Savas*, Case C-37/98 [2000] ECR I-2927

Sevince: ECJ 20 September 1990, *S. Z. Sevince v Staatssecretaris van Justitie*, Case C-192/89 [1990] ECR I-3461

Soysal: ECJ 19 February 2009, *Mehmet Soysal and Ibrahim Savatli v Bundesrepublik Deutschland*, Case C-228/06 nyr

Taflan-Met: ECJ 10 September 1996, *Z. Taflan-Met, S. Altun-Baser, E. Andal-Bugdayci v Bestuur van de Sociale Verzekeringsbank and O. Akol v Bestuur van de Nieuwe Algemene Bedrijfsvereniging*, Case C-277/94 [1996] ECR I-4085

Tetik: ECJ 23 January 1997, *Recep Tetik v Land Berlin*, Case C-171/95 [1997] ECR I-329

Tum and Dari: ECJ 20 September 2007, *The Queen, Veli Tum and Mehmet Dari v Secretary of State for the Home Department*, Case C-16/05 [2007] ECR I-7415

Yousfi: ECJ 20 April 1994, *Zoubir Yousfi v Belgian State*, Case C-58/93 [1994] ECR I-1353.

THE SOCIAL SECURITY RELATIONS BETWEEN THE EU AND THE EFTA STATES

Bernhard Zaglmayer*

INTRODUCTION

The topic of social security co-ordination between EU and non-EU countries is of particular interest as it has been rather neglected in scientific literature in the past. There is little awareness of the fact that non-EU countries are also, at least to a certain extent, affected by EC legislation although under a different framework, for instance under bi- and multilateral agreements with the EU and/or its Member States.

In such an international context, EC legislation moves away from its original form, namely the supranational character. This entails not only that certain principles of EC law no longer apply, but also that other principles which are inherent to international law become relevant and influence the impact of EC social security co-ordination. Further complications can arise given that social security co-ordination does not necessarily exist to the same extent in different bi- or multilateral agreements.

The scope of social security co-ordination outside of the territories of the EU Member States on the basis of international agreements will be illustrated in this article with the example of the relations between the EU and the EFTA States. In order to do this, a brief history of relations between the EU and EFTA will shed light on the background of the agreements. Then the nature and extent of the existing agreements that cover social security co-ordination will be explained. The core of this article will deal with the social security *acquis* of these agreements, in particular focusing on issues concerning the personal and material scope (like third country nationals and special non-contributory benefits), the development of these agreements based on case law of the European Court of Justice regarding

* Officer with the EFTA Surveillance Authority. The views expressed in this contribution are personal.

reimbursement of health care based on principles of freedom to provide services and the impact of the concept of European citizenship.

1. A BRIEF HISTORY OF EU-EFTA RELATIONS

On 4 January 1960, the European Free Trade Association (EFTA) was founded by Austria, Denmark, Norway, Portugal, Sweden, Switzerland and the UK to counterbalance the European Economic Community (EEC) (the "inner 6" and "outer 7"). Iceland joined EFTA in 1970, Finland joined in 1986 and Liechtenstein joined in 1991. Eventually, Austria, Denmark, Finland, Portugal, Sweden and the UK left EFTA to join the European Union (EU). This leaves EFTA currently with four Member States: Iceland, Liechtenstein, Norway and Switzerland.

The basis of EFTA is the EFTA Convention which has a twofold objective. Firstly, it promotes free trade between its Member States (initially covering only the trade of goods), and secondly, it is a platform for free trade arrangements between the EFTA States and third countries.

Until the mid-eighties the relation between the two trade blocks, EC and EFTA, was purely limited to the trade of goods. As of that time, EFTA States sought to strengthen their cooperation. In 1989 under the *Delors* Commission, negotiations started on a 'European Economic Space', later to become the 'European Economic Area' (EEA) envisaging a new form of association with common bodies for decision-making and administration. This idea went beyond the existing bilateral Free Trade Agreements, since it made the EFTA States an integral part of Europe's Internal Market. The EEA Agreement was then signed on 2 May 1992, but only with Iceland, Liechtenstein and Norway, as the Swiss people rejected the Agreement in a prior national referendum and opted for bilateral relations with the EU.

The EEA Agreement entered into force on 1 January 1994[1], except for Liechtenstein where it entered into force only on 1 May 1995.[2] After the accession of Austria, Finland and Sweden to the EU, the Agreement applied to only three EFTA States and the 15 Member States of the EU. The Agreement was amended after the accession of the 10 new Member States to the EU on 1 May 2004 and became

1 Agreement on the European Economic Area – Final Act – Joint Declarations – Declarations by the Governments of the Member States of the Community and the EFTA States – Arrangements – Agreed Minutes – Declarations by one or several of the Contracting Parties of the Agreement on the European Economic Area, OJ L 1 of 3 January 1994, 3–36.

2 Decision 1/95 of the EEA Council of 10 March 1995, OJ L 86 of 20 April 1995, EEA Supplement No 14 of 20 April 1995, 1; see also OJ L 140 of 23 June 1995, 30.

provisionally applicable as of that date.[3] The Enlargement Agreement entered into force on 6 December 2005.[4] Since the accession of Romania and Bulgaria to the EU on 1 January 2007, the EEA Agreement is currently provisionally applicable since 1 August 2007 in relation to those two States.[5]

Negotiations for a bilateral solution with Switzerland started in 1993 and resulted in 7 sectoral agreements ('*Bilateral I*'), one of which is the Agreement on Free Movement of Persons (FMA).[6] Article 25(2) FMA foresees the limitation of this agreement to 7 years and a possibility of renewal for an indefinite period if nothing else is notified by either Contracting Party. On 8 February 2009, the Swiss people voted in a referendum to prolong the Agreement (by 59% in favour of prolongation) and, at the same time, for its extension to Romania and Bulgaria, which will take effect as of 1 June 2009.

Currently, the EFTA Convention effectively applies mainly to the relations between Switzerland on the one hand, and the other three EFTA States on the other, since the EEA Agreement applies to all trade relations between Iceland, Liechtenstein and Norway. In April 2001, the EFTA States agreed on significant amendments to the EFTA Convention in order to modernise the Convention and to bring it up to a similar level of co-operation as between EFTA States and the European Community, especially after the latter concluded seven bilateral agreements with Switzerland ('*Bilateral I*'). The updated EFTA Convention, the 'Vaduz Convention', was signed on 21 June 2001 and entered into force on 1 June 2002. It includes several significant changes, the most important of which is the integration of the principles and rules established between the EC and the EEA EFTA States in the EEA Agreement, and between the EC and Switzerland in the EC-Swiss Bilateral Agreements.

To summarise, this results in the current legal framework for EU-EFTA relations:

- The EEA Agreement applicable to the 27 EU Member States and the 3 EEA EFTA States (Iceland, Liechtenstein and Norway);
- The EC-Swiss Bilateral Agreements applicable to 25 EU Member States and Switzerland; and
- The EFTA Convention on the bilateral relations between the 3 EEA EFTA States and Switzerland.

---

3 OJ L 130 of 29 April 2004, 11, EEA Supplement No 23 of 29 April 2004, 1.
4 OJ L 149 of 2 June 2006, 30.
5 OJ L 221 of 25 August 2007, 3.
6 Agreement between the EC and its Member States on the one hand, and the Swiss Confederation on the other, on the free movement of persons, OJ L of 30 April 2002, 6.

All frameworks contain references to social security co-ordination, but there are differences in substance.

Last, but not least, it must be noted that these agreements are not co-ordinated amongst each other. This means, for instance, that a Norwegian national who is residing in Switzerland on the basis of the EFTA Convention cannot infer any rights from the bilateral Agreement between the EC and Switzerland when migrating from Switzerland to Austria, except for those rights which are explicitly attributed to third parties of the Agreement (namely derived rights for family Members of EU or Swiss nationals). The same would apply *e.g.* for a Swiss national who is residing in Liechtenstein on the basis of the EFTA Convention and intends to migrate from Liechtenstein to Germany in the framework of the EEA Agreement.

2. THE EEA AGREEMENT

2.1. BASIC STRUCTURE AND FUNCTIONING OF THE AGREEMENT

The EEA Agreement consists of two basic separate agreements. Firstly, the EEA Agreement as such, including the enlargement agreements, consisting of the actual text of the Agreement, 49 Protocols and 22 Annexes. The EC secondary legislation that has been incorporated into the Agreement is listed per reference technique in the Annexes of the Agreement, while the Protocols mainly contain transitional provisions and procedural issues. Secondly, the Standing Committee Agreement[7] and the Surveillance and Court Agreement (SCA)[8] provide for the institutional setup in the EEA (see table of 'EEA Two-Pillar Structure' in the Annex to the article).

The development of the EEA Agreement is dynamic. This means that new EC *acquis* is regularly incorporated into the Agreement when deemed 'EEA relevant' *i.e.* when falling within the scope of the Agreement. Such incorporation is done via decisions of the Joint Committee as closely as possible to the adoption of the

---

7 The Agreement on a Standing Committee of the EFTA States amended by the Protocol Adjusting the Agreement on a Standing Committee of the EFTA States signed in Brussels on 17 March 1993 ('Adjusting Protocol'), by the Decision No 2/94/SC of the Standing Committee of the EFTA States of 10 January 1994 (OJ No L 85, 30.3.1994, p. 76 and EEA Supplement No 1, 30.3.1994, p. 14) and subsequently by the Agreement Adjusting certain Agreements between the EFTA States signed in Brussels on 29 December 1994 ('Adjusting Agreement').

8 Agreement between EFTA States on the Establishment of a Surveillance Authority and a Court of Justice, OJ L 344 of 31 January 1994, 1 and EFTA States' official gazettes.

corresponding Community legislation (Article 102(1) EEA). As the EEA EFTA States have not transferred any legislative powers to the EFTA institutions, all new legal acts (directives, regulations, *etc.*) have to be transposed into national legislation (Protocol 35 to the EEA Agreement) which is done by a ratification process according to their respective Constitutions. Only after the notification of the fulfilment of such 'constitutional requirements' of all three States do the incorporated acts become applicable in the EEA (Article 103 EEA). This procedure entails a limited application of 'direct effect' for secondary legislation in the EEA.[9] As a consequence, significant delays in the application of new legislation in the EEA might occur.

The correct implementation and application of the *acquis* is then supervised by the EFTA Surveillance Authority, which has equivalent powers to the European Commission (Article 5 SCA). It can initiate infringement proceedings against Iceland, Liechtenstein or Norway and bring cases before the EFTA Court (Article 31 SCA).[10] There is, thus, a completely independent two-pillar structure in the EEA, with both EU and EFTA institutions.[11]

2.2. THE EEA ACQUIS

The aim of the EEA Agreement is to guarantee the free movement of goods, persons, services and capital as well as equal conditions of competition and non-discrimination in all 30 EEA States. Thus, its fundamental purpose is to establish a dynamic and homogeneous European Economic Area based on common rules and equal conditions of competition (Article 1 EEA). To this end, in particular, the fundamental freedoms of the internal market are extended to the EEA EFTA States. The EEA Agreement consequently contains equivalent Internal Market provisions to those in the EC Treaty.

What are the main differences between the EU and the EEA? First of all, the EEA does not include the second and third pillars of the EU, namely Justice and Home

9 See, in particular, Case E-4/01 *Karlsson* [2002] EFTA Court Report 242 and Case E-1/07 *Fürstliches Landgericht, Liechtenstein, in criminal proceedings against A* [2007] EFTA Court Report 248. For further reading see a.o. VAN GERVEN, W., *The genesis of EEA law and principles of primacy and direct effect*, 955; BAUDENBACHER, C., *Facets of an EEA constitutional order*, 343, and BAUDENBACHER, C., *Governments before the EFTA Court*, 23.

10 For further reading see a.o. BAUDENBACHER, C., *The EFTA Court: an actor in the European judicial dialogue*, 353, and ÖRLYGSSON, T., *Iceland and the EFTA Court*, 225.

11 See also FENGER/SANCHEZ/VAN STIPHOUT, *European Free Trade Association (EFTA) and European Economic Area (EEA)*, 1.

Affairs and Common Foreign and Security Policy.[12] Furthermore, the EEA is not a customs union, but an enhanced free trade area. It is not a monetary union either and therefore does not participate in the common EURO currency. Moreover, certain policies, like agriculture and fisheries, are not part of the Agreement. Last, but not least, no equivalent concept to European citizenship exists in the EEA.

The EEA *acquis* covers also the case law of the European Court of Justice decided prior to the date of the signature of the Agreement (*cf.* Article 6 EEA and Article 3(1) SCA). Furthermore, Article 3(2) SCA specifies that in the interpretation and application of the EEA Agreement, the EFTA Surveillance Authority and the EFTA Court shall pay due account to the principles laid down by the relevant rulings by the Court of Justice given after the date of signature of the EEA Agreement. These principles apply to provisions of the EEA Agreement in so far as they are identical in substance to corresponding rules of the EC Treaty (see below point 2.3).

2.3. A BRIEF INTRODUCTION TO THE PRINCIPLE OF HOMOGENEITY

The Court of Justice of the European Communities is under no written obligation to take into account EFTA Court case law. However, the Court of Justice as well as the EFTA Court held on numerous occasions that both courts are responsible for ensuring the homogeneity of the EEA.[13] It is the presumption of this case law that identically worded provisions are to be interpreted in a homogenous, thus dynamic, way. The EFTA Court further specified that homogeneity should prevail unless specific circumstances indicate that the differences in the scope and purpose of the EEA Agreement as compared to the EC Treaty should lead to another interpretation than the one given to the EC Treaty. The president of the EFTA Court, Carl Baudenbacher, calls this process 'creative homogeneity'.[14]

---

12 The Schengen *acquis* for the EEA EFTA States is based on bilateral relations between the respective States and the EU and is not part of the EEA Agreement.

13 See *e.g.* Case C-286/02 *Bellio Fratelli* [2004] ECR I-3465, paragraph 34; Case C-452/01 *Ospelt* [2003] ECR I-9743, paragraph 29; Case E-3/98 *Rainford Towning* [1998] EFTA Court Report, 205, paragraph 20, and Case E-1/04 *Fokus Bank ASA* [2004] EFTA Court Report 15, paragraph 23.

14 BAUDENBACHER, C., *The contribution of the EFTA Court to the establishment of a homogeneous and dynamic European Economic Area.*

Where are the borders of homogeneity? The EFTA Court applies this concept rather extensively and has rejected arguments by the Governments that a dynamic development of the EEA is for the Governments in the Joint Committee and not for the Court. In this context, one can observe that the case law of the EFTA Court is characterised by two main lines. On the one hand, the EFTA Court normally makes a statement of principle that it will follow the agreement as it is and not apply a new EC rule by analogy. On the other hand, with regard to the outcome, the Court *de facto* applies a homogeneity approach that places emphasis on EC law as it stands at the time of the decision rather than as it stood at the time of the signature of the Agreement.[15] However, no judgment has yet had a result that could solely be reached by taking account of provisions in the EC Treaty which were inserted after the signing of the EEA Agreement.[16]

2.4. SOCIAL SECURITY CO-ORDINATION UNDER THE EEA AGREEMENT

Article 29 EEA is the equivalent provision to Article 42 EC serving as legal basis for Regulations 1408/71 and 574/72.[17] It refers to Annex VI to the Agreement, where the Regulations have been incorporated at points 1 and 2, including the amending regulations. Point 3 of Annex VI lists all Decisions and Recommendations of the Administrative Commission on Social Security for Migrant Workers having been incorporated into the EEA Agreement and to be duly taken into account. Furthermore, Annex VI contains the entries into the Annexes to Regulation 1408/71 and 574/72 for Iceland, Liechtenstein and Norway.

Equally, part of the EEA Agreement is the case law of the EFTA Court, where so far five cases in the field of social security were decided:

---

15 FENGER, N., *Limits to a Dynamic Homogeneity between EC Law and EEA Law*, 144.

16 For further reading see a.o. BAUDENBACHER, C., *Der EFTA Gerichtshof, das EWR-Abkommen und die Fortentwicklungen des EG-Vertrags*, 63; FORMAN, J., *The EEA Agreement five years on: Dynamic homogeneity in practise and its implementation by the two EEA Courts*, 751; GRAVER, H-P., *The EFTA Court and the Court of Justice of the EC: Legal homogeneity at stake?*, 31, and GRAVER, H-P, *Mission impossible: supranationality and national legal autonomy in the EEA Agreement*, 73.

17 Regulation (EEC) No 1408/71 of the Council of 14 June 1971 *on the application of social security schemes to employed persons and their families moving within the Community*, OJ L 149 of 5 July 1971, 1; consolidated version, OJ L 28 of 30 January 1997, 1, and Council Regulation (EEC) No 574/72 of 21 March 1972 *laying down the procedure for implementing regulation (EEC) No 1408/71 on the application of social security schemes to employed persons, to self employed persons and to members of their families moving within the Community*, OJ L 74 of 27 March 1972, 1.

- Case E-3/04 *Tsomakas Athanasios,* concerning the posting of workers[18];
- Case E-3/05 *ESA v Norway* ("Finnmark benefit"), concerning the export of regional family benefits[19];
- Case E-5/06 *ESA v Liechtenstein* ("Helplessness allowance"), concerning special non-contributory benefits[20];
- Case E-4/07 *Jón Gunnar Þorkelsson v Gildi-lífeyrissjóður* ("Gildi Pension Fund") concerning the co-ordination of projected pension rights for funded pension schemes under Regulation 1408/71[21]; and
- Joined Cases E-11/07 *Rindal* & E-1/08 *Slinning,* concerning the right to reimbursement of experimental medical treatment abroad based on the provisions to freely provide services.[22]

Even though nearly the whole EC *acquis* has been incorporated into the EEA Agreement, some particularities exist.

2.4.1. Third Country Nationals (TCN)

The EEA Agreement is explicitly restricted to nationals of the EU and EEA EFTA States. Therefore no legislation concerning TCN, including Directive 2003/109 *on the status of third-country nationals as long-term residents*[23] and, of particular importance for social security co-ordination, Regulation 859/03 *extending the provisions of Regulation 1408/71 to TCN*[24], is part of the EEA Agreement and thus not applicable in the EEA. As a consequence, the extension of the application of Regulation 1408/71 to TCN is limited in the EEA.

However, there are situations when TCN fall within the ambit of EEA law, namely when being a family member of an EEA national. This has particular consequences in the field of health care.

Regulation 631/04 introducing the European Health Insurance Card (EHIC) has been incorporated into the EEA Agreement, and is applicable in the EEA since

18 Case E-3/04 *Tsomakas Athanasios and Others* [2004] EFTA Court Report 97.
19 Case E-3/05 *EFTA Surveillance Authority v Norway* [2006] EFTA Court Report 104.
20 Case E-5/06 *EFTA Surveillance Authority v The Principality of Liechtenstein* [2007] EFTA Court Report 298.
21 Case E-4/07 *Jón Gunnar Þorkelsson v Gildi-lífeyrissjóður* [2008] EFTA Court Report 5.
22 Joined Cases E-11/07 *Rindal* & E-1/08 *Slinning,* judgment of 19 December 2008, not yet published.
23 Council Directive 2003/109/EC of 25 November 2003 *concerning the status of third-country nationals who are long-term residents,* OJ L 16 of 23 January 2004, 44.
24 Council Regulation (EC) No 859/2003 of 14 May 2003 *extending the provisions of Regulation (EEC) No 1408/71 and Regulation (EEC) No 574/72 to nationals of third countries who are not already covered by those provisions solely on the ground of their nationality,* OJ L 124 of 20 May 2003, 1.

1 January 2006.[25] While TCN in the EU Member States have a right to health care based on Regulation 859/03, such an independent right does not exist for TCN in the EEA EFTA States. TCN are only granted derived rights as family members of nationals of one of the EEA States and can only be issued an EHIC in Liechtenstein, Iceland and Norway on this basis.

A problem might occur when a TCN intends to use the EHIC issued by an EU Member State based on Regulation 859/03 for treatment in one of the EEA EFTA States. On the one hand, strictly legally speaking, the EHIC can only be used in EEA EFTA States, if it has been obtained as a derived right, and not when the right is based on Regulation 859/03. The service provider could thus refuse the EHIC. On the other hand, it is unrealistic to expect a doctor to first establish the nationality of a patient and then, in case the patient turns out to have a third-country nationality, to ask for a certificate stating the person is a family member of an EEA national, to make sure that he can accept the EHIC from the patient.

Therefore, there will be cases where the EHIC is used illegally due to a lack of knowledge of the patient and/or the lack of control from the service provider. The consequence would be that the competent state is not obliged to reimburse the host state for the treatment, due to the lack of a legal basis. These cases will, however, rather be the exception, and it can be expected from the States involved to handle such cases in a pragmatic way.

2.4.2. Special Non-Contributory Benefits

As stated above, Article 3(2) SCA specifies that in the interpretation and application of the EEA Agreement the EFTA Surveillance Authority and the EFTA Court shall pay due account to the principles laid down by the relevant rulings by the Court of Justice given after the date of signature of the EEA Agreement. The extent to which this applies to special non-contributory benefits, shall be illustrated using the recent judgment of the EFTA Court in Case E-5/06 concerning the Liechtenstein helplessness allowance (*Hilflosenentschädigung*).[26]

Even though the relevant judgments of *Jauch*, *Hosse* and *Commission v Council and Parliament* were handed down in 2001 and 2006 respectively, thus after the

---

25 Regulation (EC) No 631/2004 of the European Parliament and of the Council of 31 March 2004 *amending Council Regulation (EEC) No 1408/71 on the application of social security schemes to employed persons, to self-employed persons and to members of their families moving within the Community, and Council Regulation (EEC) No 574/72 laying down the procedure for implementing Regulation (EEC) No 1408/71, in respect of the alignment of rights and the simplification of procedures*, OJ L 100 of 6 April 2004, 1.

26 Case E-5/06 *EFTA Surveillance Authority v The Principality of Liechtenstein*, cited above.

date of signature of the EEA Agreement, the EFTA Court applied them fully to the Liechtenstein care benefit which was very similar to the one at stake in *Hosse*.[27] This happened before Regulation 647/05 codifying the Court's case law was incorporated in the EEA Agreement.[28]

The Liechtenstein Government argued during the proceedings before the EFTA Court, amongst other things, that it acknowledged the principle of homogeneity and the dynamic character of the EEA Agreement. On the other hand, Annex IIa to Regulation 1408/71 was of great concern during the negotiations for joining the EEA Agreement. Liechtenstein even decided to change the character of the benefit from contributory to non-contributory in order to have it listed in Annex IIa and therefore not be obliged to export it. This non-exportability was a *conditio sine qua non* for accession to the EEA. At that time, Annex IIa was considered as having a constitutive effect, meaning that benefits listed therein were recognised as being non-exportable. This can be derived from the fact that, until 2001, the Court of Justice did not question whether the listing of a benefit in Annex IIa was compatible with Community law. Liechtenstein referred in this respect to *Snares, Partridge* and *Swaddling*.[29] Therefore, according to Liechtenstein, the Agreement has to be interpreted in this respect in accordance with the principle laid down in Article 26 of the Vienna Convention of the Law of Treaties: *pacta sunt servanda*.[30]

The EFTA Court could however not see the relevance of this argument, and dealt with this issue rather briefly stating that "*in its interpretation of the EEA Agreement, the Court cannot be bound by mere expectations of the Contracting Parties as to the exact content of the obligations of the parties*". Moreover, according to the Court, no explicit declaration or any derogation regarding the helplessness allowance exist and Liechtenstein would, therefore, be in the same position as all other Contracting Parties.[31] Thus, the Liechtenstein helplessness allowance has to be classified as a sickness benefit and co-ordinated under Title III, Chapter 1 of Regulation 1408/71.

---

27 Case C-215/99 *Jauch* [2001] ECR I-1901; Case C-286/03 *Hosse* [2006] ECR I-1771 and Case C-299/05 *Commission v Parliament and Council* [2007] ECR I-8695.

28 Regulation (EC) No 647/2005 of the European Parliament and of the Council of 13 April 2005 *amending Council Regulations (EEC) No 1408/71 on the application of social security schemes to employed persons, to self-employed persons and to members of their families moving within the Community and (EEC) No 574/72 laying down the procedure for implementing Regulation (EEC) No 1408/71*, OJ L 117 of 4 May 2005, 1.

29 Case C-20/96 *Snares* [1997] ECR I-6057, paragraph 32; Case C-297/96 *Partridge* [1998] ECR I-3467, at paragraph 33 and Case C-90/97 *Swaddling* [1999] ECR I-1075, paragraph 24.

30 Case E-5/06 *EFTA Surveillance Authority v The Principality of Liechtenstein*, cited above, paragraph 46.

31 Ibid, paragraph 63.

This example shows that the EFTA Court follows its established principle in *Rainford-Towning* that homogeneity should prevail unless specific circumstances indicate that the differences in the scope and purpose of the EEA Agreement as compared to the EC Treaty should lead to another interpretation than the one given in the EC.[32]

As a consequence, Norway also agreed to delete two entries from Annex IIa. Iceland does not have any entry in Annex IIa. With Joint Committee Decision 102/2008 of 26 September 2008, Regulation 647/05 was incorporated into the EEA Agreement.

2.4.3. *Reimbursement of Cross-Border Medical Treatment Based on the Provision of Services*

In the light of the above reasoning of the EFTA Court, it is not surprising that the *Kohll & Decker* doctrine established by the Court of Justice since 1998 is also fully part of the EEA *acquis*.[33] As there is Article 36 EEA, which is practically identical to Article 49 EC concerning the free provision of services, the Surveillance Authority and also the EFTA Court apply the case law of the Court of Justice to its full extent.

Only recently, in a judgment delivered on 19 December 2008, did the EFTA Court give an advisory opinion on questions referred to it from two Norwegian courts regarding the interpretation of the rules on free movement of services in the health care sector.[34] It is not necessary to elaborate on all issues at stake in detail – rather it is revealing enough to highlight that, based on the judgment of the Court of Justice in *Smits-Peerbooms*[35], the EFTA Court concluded that it was compatible with EEA law to refuse coverage of costs for non-recognised (test or experimental) treatment abroad when there is no entitlement to such treatment in the home state.[36]

One point of special interest should however be mentioned here. The EFTA Court referred to the principle established by the Court of Justice that a prioritisation of national treatment in a hospital can only be justified "*as long as the State provides the treatment within a medically justifiable time limit and on the condition that the*

32 Case E-3/98 *Rainford Towning, cited above*, paragraph 20.
33 Case C-158/96 *Kohll* [1998] ECR I-1931 and Case C-120/95 *Decker* [1998] ECR I-1831.
34 Joined Cases E-11/07 *Rindal* & E-1/08 *Slinning*, judgment of 19 December 2008, not yet published.
35 Case C-157/99 *Smits and Peerbooms* [2001] ECR I-5473.
36 Joined Cases E-11/07 *Rindal* & E-1/08 *Slinning*, judgment of 19 December 2008, not yet published, paragraphs 58–61.

domestic treatment is equally effective as the treatment which the patient seeks abroad".[37] The Court however continued stating in the next paragraph that "*when it is established, according to international medicine, that the treatment abroad is* indeed more effective (emphasis added) *the State may no longer justify prioritising its own offer of treatment.*[38]

This conclusion of the EFTA Court would mean that a patient can seek reimbursement on the basis of Article 36 EEA not only when the time limit exceeds what may be termed as medically acceptable, which is settled case law, but also which is the novelty when the treatment is more advanced or effective. No indications are given by the Court as to what would constitute an 'indeed more effective' treatment, *e.g.* to be considerably or manifestly more effective.

This case is of particular interest, as this approach was already applied once in the 1970s by the Court of Justice in the *Pierik* cases based on Article 22 of Regulation 1408/71.[39] According to the judgments, Member States were obliged to grant an authorisation allowing insured persons to receive treatment in another Member State if the treatment was more efficient in that State. It does not come as much of a surprise that the Member States were not particularly enthusiastic about this state of affairs. Article 22(2) second subparagraph of Regulation 1408/71 was therefore amended by Article 1(1) of Regulation 2793/81 to ensure that the home State had sufficient discretion to refuse authorisation.[40] It is interesting that the EFTA Court has now reached the same result on the basis of the provisions to provide services.

However, holding that the rights to health care created by virtue of Article 49 EC could be more extensive than what a patient would be entitled to in the home State (*e.g.* where the treatment in the host State is more advanced) in the author's view appears to presuppose that an independent right to state funding of medical treatment could be derived from the EC Treaty. The case law of the Court of Justice to date does not appear to base itself on that. Quite the opposite, the starting point is the legislation of the home State and whether, by virtue of that legislation, the patient has a right to a given treatment within the confines of its social security system. It is only once the national legislator has granted such a

---

37 Case C-157/99 *Smits and Peerbooms* [2001] ECR I-5473, paragraph 103, and Case C-372/04 *Watts* [2006] ECR I-4325, paragraph 120.

38 Joined Cases E-11/07 *Rindal* & E-1/08 *Slinning*, cited above, paragraphs 84–85.

39 Cases 117/77 *Pierik I* [1978] ECR 825 and 182/78 *Pierik II* [1979] ECR 1977.

40 See Article 1 of Council Regulation (EEC) No 2793/81 of 17 September 1981 *amending Regulation (EEC) No 1408/71 on the application of social security schemes to employed persons and their families moving within the Community and Regulation (EEC) No 574/72 fixing the procedure for implementing Regulation (EEC) No 1408/71*, OJ L 275 of 29 September 1981, 1. Interestingly, the recitals to the Regulation made no reference to the *Pierik* judgments.

right that the patient may, on the basis of EC law, enjoy to the right to receive that kind of treatment in another Member State. The only way to derive a more extensive right to health care from EC law would be to consider the right to health care to be a fundamental right. To date, the Court of Justice has refrained from doing so.

It remains to be seen whether the Court of Justice will take up this line in any future rulings; or whether maybe even the European legislator will take up this new approach in the context of the new proposal for a Directive on patient rights.[41]

2.4.4. The Concept of European Citizenship in the EEA

There is no equivalent provision to the concept of European citizenship in the EEA Agreement. As for the question of the interpretation of the EEA *acquis* in the light of citizenship rights, the EFTA Court has not yet taken a stand. It is however of great interest to consider whether the EFTA Court would apply the case law of the Court of Justice to the citizenship concept in the field of social security.[42]

To answer this question, one has to distinguish between two issues. First of all, whether the facts are related to migrant workers or purely to non-active persons. In the latter case, there is clearly no room for application of citizenship rights in the EEA. In respect of active persons, one could imagine that the EFTA Court would look into the case and see whether the result of the respective case before the Court of Justice could be reached by applying the principle of non-discrimination together with the relevant secondary legislation based on the principle of homogeneity and the dynamic character of the EEA Agreement.

Another aspect is the interpretation of 'new' legislation that is being incorporated into the EEA Agreement, which is also based on citizenship rights, in the light of the principle of homogeneity and the dynamic character of the EEA Agreement, for example Directive 2004/38 on residence rights.[43]

---

41 Prosopal for a Directive of the European Parliament and of the Council *on the application of patients' rights in cross-border healthcare*, COM/2008/414 final.

42 See *e.g.* Case C-224/98 *D'Hoop* [2002] ECR I-6191; Case C-184/99 *Grzelczyk* [2001] ECR I-6193; Case C-138/02 *Collins* [2004] ECR I-2703; Case C-456/02 *Trojani* [2004] ECR I-7573; Case C-209/03 *Bidar* [2005] ECR I-2119; Case C-258/04 *Joannidis* [2005] ECR I-8275; Case C-406/04 *De Cuyper* [2006] ECR I-6947; Case C-192/05 *Tas-Hagen and Tas* [2006] ECR I-10451; Case C-499/06 *Nerkowska* [2008] ECR I-3993 and Case C-221/07 *Zablocka-Weyermüller*, not yet published.

43 Directive 2004/38/EC of the European Parliament and of the Council of 29 April 2004 *on the right of citizens of the Union and their family members to move and reside freely within the territory of the Member States amending Regulation (EEC) No 1612/68 and repealing Directives and*, OJ L 158 of 30 April 2004, 77.

The concept of European citizenship might thus potentially affect the EEA Agreement – at least this possibility cannot be categorically excluded. It is however also clear that the concept will not reach the same extent as in the EU.

3. THE EC-SWISS BILATERAL AGREEMENT ON THE FREE MOVEMENT OF PERSONS (FMA)

3.1. BASIC STRUCTURE OF THE FMA AND ITS SCOPE

The EC-Swiss Bilateral Agreement is the replacement for the EEA Agreement, which was rejected in a referendum by the Swiss people in 1992. The main reason for the refusal was opposition to direct extension of the EU *acquis* to the EEA Agreement and a supranational jurisdiction in the form of the EFTA Court.[44] The FMA is therefore based on the principle of the equivalence of the legal systems of the signatories.

It consists, similarly to the EEA Agreement, of the text of the Agreement (25 Articles), including one Additional Protocol for the enlargement of the FMA to the 10 new EU Member States as of 1 April 2006, and 3 Annexes where the references to EC secondary legislation can be found.[45] The Agreement does not include an additional agreement on the institutional setup, as there is no two-pillar structure like in the EEA. Article 14 FMA establishes the basis for a Joint Committee consisting of representatives of the Contracting Parties which is "*responsible for the management and proper application*" of the FMA.

The FMA contains the basic EC *acquis* on the free movement of (natural) persons, including provisions on the free movement of workers, freedom to provide services and the right to establishment. It is decisive for the application of this Agreement to clarify its interpretation in accordance with EC law where, according to settled case law of the Court of Justice, free movement of persons consists not only of the free movement of workers, but also the freedom to provide services and the right to establishment.[46] There are, however, clear deviations from the EU *acquis*. The particularities affecting the field of social security co-ordination will be discussed below.

---

44 IMHOF, E., *Das Freizügigkeitsabkommen EG – Schweiz und seine Auslegungsmethode*, Teil 1, ZESAR 4/07, 155.

45 A second Additional Protocol will be added as of 1 June 2009, to extend the Agreement to Romania and Bulgaria.

46 See. *e.g.* Case C-106/91 *Ramrath* [1992] ECR I-3351, paragraphs 25–27, and Case 279/80 *Webb* [1981] ECR 3305, paragraph 14.

The aim of the Agreement is to grant a right of entry, residence for workers and for non-active persons, to grant equal access to work, to facilitate the provision of services and non-discrimination with regard to living, employment and working conditions (Article 1 FMA). To this end, Articles 2–9 FMA contain the substantive provisions. The remaining provisions of the Agreement regulate transitional measures and procedural issues.

According to Article 16(1) FMA, the Contracting Parties shall take all measures necessary to ensure that rights and obligations equivalent to those contained in the legal acts of the EC, to which reference is made, in order to attain the objective of the Agreement. This provision obliges Switzerland to incorporate the *acquis* of the Agreement in its national legislation. As it is a monistic state, the provisions of the FMA are directly applicable and have priority over national legislation, as long as they fulfil the requirements for 'direct effect' as set out by the European Court of Justice.[47]

The *acquis* of the FMA covers also the case law of the Court of Justice before the date of signature (21 June 1999). Article 16(2) FMA clarifies that in as far as the application of the Agreement is concerned, case law of the Court of Justice after the date of signature shall be brought to the attention of Switzerland. To ensure the good functioning of the FMA, the Joint Committee shall at the request of either Contracting Party determine the implications of such case law. In other words, the Joint Committee decides which case law will be incorporated into the Agreement.

In the light of the above, it can be concluded that contrary to the EEA Agreement, the FMA is not a dynamic but a static agreement, with the option of amendments to new legislation or case law via the Joint Committee.

3.2. THE FMA AND ITS INTERPRETATION

Any revision of the FMA or dispute concerning the FMA has to be brought before the Joint Committee (Articles 18 and 19 FMA). It is however also settled case law of the Court of Justice that it has jurisdiction to interpret the provisions of mixed agreements relating to powers under primary law, since such powers form an integral part of the Community legal system. In the absence of a specific statement,

47 See, to that extent, Case 12/86 *Demirel* [1987] ECR 3719, paragraph 14, and the Opinion of AG Colomer in Case C-399/05 *Zentralbetriebsrat*, struck out of the list, paragraph 33.

that jurisdiction is based on Article 220 EC, which provides that the Court is charged with ensuring that Community law is observed.[48]

The establishment of a special institutional framework – the Joint Committee – does not preclude the intervention of the Court since the duties of that committee, which are to take responsibility for 'the management and proper application of the Agreement' and to hear disputes concerning the application of the Agreement, are not adversely affected when a court of one of the contracting parties relies, in proceedings, on an unconditional and precise provision or refers a question for a preliminary ruling.[49] Thus, the Court of Justice is competent to act, in particular when a question by a national court of an EU Member State is referred.

According to Advocate General Colomer, interpretations from the Court of Justice would have to take into account Article 31 of the Vienna Convention on the Law of Treaties of 23 May 1969, stating that account must also be taken of the wording, purpose and nature of the treaty, and moreover the principle that, although the will of the parties constitutes an interpretative guide (the subjective construction), an overall approach which takes account of the purpose and scheme is essential.[50]

In legal practice, however, the Swiss courts play the main role for the application of the case law of the Court of Justice at national level, in particular the Federal Court which decides as final instance, since no access to the European Court of Justice for advisory opinions is foreseen in the FMA.

3.3. THE FMA AND SOCIAL SECURITY CO-ORDINATION

Article 8 FMA lists the principles of social security co-ordination like in Article 42 EC and refers to Annex II where the incorporated EC secondary legislation is listed by the use of reference technique, including the entries in the Annexes to Regulation 1408/71 for Switzerland. There is also a Protocol to Annex II to the FMA, listing amongst others exceptions to specific provisions of Regulation 1408/71.

48 Case 12/86 *Demirel* [1987] ECR 3719, paragraph 7; Case 181/73 *Haegeman* [1974] ECR 449, paragraph 6, and Opinion of AG Colomer in Case C-399/05 *Zentralbetriebsrat*, struck out of the list, paragraph 29.

49 Case 104/81 *Kupferberg* [1982] ECR 3641, paragraphs 19 and 20.

50 Opinion of AG Colomer in Case C-339/05 *Zentralbetriebsrat*, struck out of the list, paragraphs 34 and 51.

Until today, the Joint Committee has amended the social security *acquis* of the FMA only twice, namely in order to introduce the European Health Insurance Card (EHIC) and other miscellaneous amendments.[51]

3.3.1. Particularities for the Co-Ordination of Sickness and Unemployment Benefits

Detailed entries of Switzerland into Annex VI to Regulation 1408/71 concern the provision of sickness benefits. Under the terms of the FMA, people who live in an EU State and work in Switzerland are obliged to take out Swiss health insurance. This also applies to their dependants who are not economically active. There are many exceptions to the rule, namely for people in gainful employment and their dependants who are living in Austria, Finland (only for dependants), France, Germany or Italy. They may be exempted from compulsory health insurance if they can prove that they are insured in their state of residence. Dependants who are not in gainful employment and who are living in Denmark, Portugal, Spain, Sweden or the UK automatically come under the insurance schemes of the corresponding state and are exempt from compulsory Swiss health insurance.

Frontier workers who are insured in Switzerland have a choice as regards treatment for illness or accidents at work. They can be treated either in their state of residence or in the state in which they work. The same choice applies to dependants who are not in gainful employment and insured in Switzerland, if they are resident in Austria, Belgium, Germany, France or the Netherlands.

The tables below give an overview of the different possibilities concerning sickness insurance[52]:

1. **Employed or self-employed persons and their family members**

Category of persons	Member State of residence	Sickness insurance
Employed or self-employed persons who are subject to Swiss social security legislation	Germany, Austria, France, Italy	**Right of option:** Insurance in Switzerland or in Member State of residence

51 Decision 2/2003 of the EU-Swiss Joint Committee of 15 July 2003, OJ L 187 of 26 July 2003, 55, and Decision 1/2006 of the EU-Swiss Joint Committee of 6 July 2006, OJ L 270 of 29 September 2006, 67.

52 Source: website of European Commission, DG Employment, Unit E/3, Social Security Co-ordination: http://ec.europa.eu/employment_social/social_security_schemes/switzerland_en.html.

Non-active family members of persons mentioned above, and of employed or self-employed persons who reside and are insured in Switzerland	Germany, Austria, France, Italy, Finland	**Right of option:** Insurance in Switzerland or in Member State of residence
	Denmark, Spain, Hungary, Portugal, Sweden, United Kingdom	Insurance in Member State of residence – automatic exemption from Swiss insurance

2. Pensioners and their family members

Category of persons	Member State of residence	Sickness insurance
Pensioners who receive a Swiss pension (alone, or with other pensions) and for whom Switzerland should be the competent Member State	Germany, Austria, France, Italy, Portugal	**Right of option:** Insurance in Switzerland or in Member State of residence
Non-active family members of pensioners who reside and are insured in Switzerland	Germany, Austria, France, Italy, Finland	**Right of option:** Insurance in Switzerland or in Member State of residence
	Denmark, Portugal, Sweden, United Kingdom	Insurance in Member State of residence – automatic exemption from Swiss insurance

3. Unemployed persons and their family members

Category of persons	Member State of residence	Sickness insurance
Recipients of Swiss unemployment benefits	Germany, Austria, France, Italy	**Right of option:** Insurance in Switzerland or in Member State of residence
Non-active family members of recipients of Swiss unemployment benefits	Germany, Austria, France, Italy, Finland	**Right of option:** Insurance in Switzerland or in Member State of residence
	Denmark, Spain, Hungary, Portugal, Sweden, United Kingdom	Insurance in Member State of residence – automatic exemption from Swiss insurance

Special transitional arrangements for unemployment benefits are based on Article 3 of Annex II in conjunction with the Additional Protocol to Annex II. This transitional period extends until 31 May 2009 for the EU 15, and Malta and Cyprus. For the other new EU Member States, this period is extended until 30 April 2011.[53]

[53] See point 5 of Annex II to the Enlargement Protocol of the FMA.

During this transition, employed workers in Switzerland with a residence permit of less than 1 year have to pay unemployment contributions in Switzerland for the minimum period required under Swiss legislation, without taking into consideration payments in other EU Member States. This is simply a restriction of the aggregation of insurance periods. If the migrant does not have sufficient periods under the Swiss system (currently 6 months; and 12 months in case of recurrent unemployment), the EU Member State of origin becomes responsible (but Swiss insurance periods are taken into account). A migrant worker is however always entitled to Swiss benefits in the case of insolvency of the employer.

3.3.2. *Third Country Nationals*

The Agreement covers only citizens of an EU Member State or Switzerland who are gainfully employed and students, and the respective family members. Legislation concerning TCN *i.e.* Directive 2003/109 *on the status of third-country nationals as long-term residents* and Regulation 859/03 *extending the provisions of Regulation 1408/71 to TCN*, is not part of the FMA. Those persons who are not gainfully employed and not of Swiss nationality or a nationality of an EU Member State are not covered by the FMA, unless they are family members or surviving dependants. They will fall under the remaining inter-state agreements. Thus, the extension of the application of Regulation 1408/71 to TCN is as limited as in the EEA Agreement.

As mentioned above, Regulation 631/04 introducing the EHIC has been incorporated into the Agreement by Joint Committee Decision 1/2006. It is enough to state that the problem with the EHIC exists as much for Switzerland as for the three EEA EFTA States, where such a card can only be obtained by a TCN as a derived right (see above point 2.4.1).

3.3.3. *Special Non-Contributory Benefits*

Switzerland has an entry in Annex IIa to Regulation 1408/71 which is of interest. It is the helplessness allowance (*Hilflosenentschädigung*). It was introduced into Annex IIa by Joint Committee Decision 2/2003 of 15 July 2003, retroactively as of 1 June 2002. This benefit was the model for the Liechtenstein benefit with the same name that was held as being a sickness benefit by the EFTA Court, mainly based on the case law of the Court of Justice in *Jauch, Hosse* and *Comission v Council and Parliament.*[54]

Article 16(2) FMA clarifies that in as far as the application of the FMA is concerned, case law of the Court of Justice after the date of signature shall be brought to the attention of Switzerland. It is therefore of interest to consider how the

54 Case E-5/06 *EFTA Surveillance Authority v The Principality of Liechtenstein*, cited above.

FMA applies this case law which emerged after the date of signature of the Agreement, 21 June 1999.

The Swiss Federal Court thus had to assess whether an entry in Annex IIa of Regulation 1408/71 was of a constitutive character, as in *Snares*, *Partridge* and *Swaddling*[55] (pre-1999 *acquis*), or whether the material characteristics also had to be tested, as later decided in *Jauch* and follow-up cases (post-1999 *acquis*).[56]

In order to decide this, it had to define the notion of 'new' case law, as referred to in Article 16(2) FMA. It was rather obvious that the creation of new principles or the response to a legal question which has never before been referred to the Court of Justice can be classified as a 'new' judgment. But what about cases where previously developed principles are applied to new provisions? Moreover, would this also include case law which is merely restating previous judgments more precisely?

In its judgment of 24 July 2006, the Swiss Federal Court referred to *Snares*, *Partridge* and *Swaddling* as cases whose main message was that the listing of the benefits at stake into Annex IIa made them special non-contributory benefits.[57] The nature of the benefits as such was not at stake. Not so in *Jauch*, where the Advocate General Albers, for the first time, questioned whether the benefits in Annex IIa had to stand a material test. On this basis, the Court of Justice started to systematically test the nature of benefits in Annex IIa. From this, the Court concluded that the Court of Justice has rather changed its jurisprudence in *Jauch* than stated already known principles more precisely. Furthermore, the judgment of *Molenaar*[58] from 1998 would not alter the result, since in this case the benefit was not listed in Annex IIa to Regulation 1408/71.[59]

Moreover, according to the Swiss Federal Court, it has to be kept in mind that the Joint Committee decided in 2003 (two years after the judgment in *Jauch*) to include the Swiss helplessness allowance in Annex IIa, being fully aware of the case law at that time. Consequently, there is no obligation to export the helplessness allowance in the framework of the FMA.[60]

In the light of the above, such an obligation could only be imposed if the Joint Committee had decided to incorporate Regulation 647/05 codifying the case law

55 Cases C-20/96 *Snares*, cited above; C-297/96 *Partridge*, cited above and C-90/97 *Swaddling*, cited above.

56 The findings in the *Jauch* judgment were confirmed in Case C-43/99 *Leclere and Deaconescu* [2001] ECR I-4265, paragraph 35, and Case C-286/03 *Hosse*, cited above, paragraph 22.

57 Swiss Federal Court, Case I 667/05, judgment of 24 July 2006 (BGE 132 V 423)(IT).

58 Case C-160/96 *Molenaar* [1998] ECR I-843.

59 Swiss Federal Court, Case I 667/05, cited above, point 9.4.1–9.4.3.

60 Ibid, point 9.5.3.

of the Court of Justice in regard to special non-contributory benefits.[61] It remains to be seen, when Regulation 883/04 is incorporated into the FMA, whether this non-exportability can be upheld, given that the new Co-ordination Regulation contains the *acquis* of Regulation 647/05.[62]

Therefore, based on the principle of reciprocity of international agreements, the EU Member States would also not have to export their special non-contributory benefits which were listed at the time of signature of the Agreement in Annex IIa to Regulation 1408/71.

3.3.4. *Reimbursement of Cross-Border Medical Treatment Based on the Provision of Services*

Next to the co-ordination regulations, the provisions of free movement of goods (Article 28 EC) and freedom to provide services (Article 49 EC) of the EC Treaty are of relevance for the reimbursement of medical treatment abroad. The Court of Justice held in the seminal *Kohll*[63] and *Decker*[64] cases that the reimbursement of cross-border health care can also be based directly on Treaty provisions. The Court delivered several judgments on this issue in the past 10 years, and on this basis the Commission initiated new legislation in order to codify and clarify the abundant case law in this field.[65] As a result, a proposal for a Directive on patients' rights in cross-border healthcare was published on 2 August 2008.[66]

Until such a directive is adopted in the EC (and eventually made part of the FMA), the case law of the Court of Justice is to be applied. In relation to Switzerland, the main problem with the case law is not related to old and new jurisprudence as in the case of special non-contributory benefits. The judgments in *Kohll* and *Decker* were handed down before the signature of the FMA, and the follow-up cases of *Smits-Peerbooms* and *Müller-Fauré* were only stating findings

---

61 Regulation (EC) No 647/2005 of the European Parliament and of the Council of 13 April 2005 *amending Council Regulations (EEC) No 1408/71 on the application of social security schemes to employed persons, to self-employed persons and to members of their families moving within the Community and (EEC) No 574/72 laying down the procedure for implementing Regulation (EEC) No 1408/71*, OJ L 117 of 4 May 2005, 1.

62 Regulation (EC) No 883/2004 of the European Parliament and of the Council of 29 April 2004 *on the co-ordination of social security systems*, OJ L 166 of 30 April 2004, 1.

63 Case C-158/96 *Kohll*, cited above.

64 Case C-120/95 *Decker*, cited above.

65 See *Consultation regarding Community action on health services* of 26 September 2006, SEC (2006) 1195/4.

66 Proposal for a Directive of the European Parliament and of the Council *on the application of patients' rights in cross-border healthcare*, COM/2008/414 final.

more precisely.[67] Most of the 'new' questions raised in later case law like *Inizan, Watts,* and *Leichtle*[68], which are mostly decisive for cross-border hospital treatment, are not as relevant for Switzerland given that Swiss national legislation is more beneficial than the concepts developed in those cases.[69]

The problem lies on a more general level, namely whether the *acquis* of the FMA has the same content in the field of free provision of services as Article 49 EC in order to equally apply the relevant rulings of the Court of Justice on cross-border health care. This is of particular relevance for out-patient treatment.

The FMA refers in the following Articles to the free provision of services. Article 1(b) states that one objective of the Agreement is to facilitate the provision of services and to liberalise the provision of short-term services. Article 5 FMA provides that service providers shall have the right to provide a service in the territory of the other contracting party for a period not exceeding 90 days per calendar year enjoying the right to entry and residence. The same applies to the service recipient (see Article 5, paragraph 3, in conjunction with Article 23 of Annex I to the FMA). Article 17 of Annex I to the FMA prohibits any restriction of cross-border service provision for services of less than 90 days.

Several cases were put forward to the Swiss Federal Court which addressed the problem of Swiss administrations refusing to reimburse out-patient treatment in EU Member States, because the patients had not requested or received prior authorisation.[70] The Court always stated in general that one has to take into account that the case law based on Article 49 EC is part of the basic principles of free movement which realise the Internal Market in the EC. No such Internal Market is part of the *sectoral* Agreement with Switzerland. In substance, the Court referred to the scope of the provisions addressing the freedom to provide services within the FMA framework and concluded that application of the service provision is restricted. In this respect, it particularly referred to the fact that services are limited to a maximum duration of 90 days per calendar year and that the emphasis of the FMA lies in granting entry and residence rights. Moreover, a *Joint Declaration on the general liberalisation of the provision of services* in the

---

67 Case C-157/99 *Smits and Peerbooms* [2001] ECR I-5473 and Case C-385/99 *Müller-Fauré* [2003] ECR I-4509.

68 Case C-56/01 *Inizan* [2003] ECR I-12403; Case C-372/04 *Watts* [2006] ECR I-4325 and Case C-8/02 *Leichtle*, [2004] ECR I-2641.

69 IMHOF, E., *Das Freizügigkeitsabkommen EG – Schweiz und seine Auslegungsmethode*, Teil 2, ZESAR 5–6/07, 220.

70 Swiss Federal Court, Case 8C_192/2007 (BGE 133 V 624)(IT), judgment of 22 October 2007; confirmed by Case I 601/06 (DE), judgment of 12 March 2008 and 9C_479/2008 (DE), judgment of 30 December 2008, paragraph.

Final Act to the FMA[71] states the intention to commence as soon as possible negotiations for liberalisation based on the *acquis communautaire*.[72]

In the light of the above, the Swiss Federal Court held that the case law of the Court of Justice on cross-border health care without restrictions is going beyond the objective of the FMA, and Switzerland is therefore not bound by it.

Consequently, the application of the principles established in *Kohll* and the follow-up case law requires a decision of the Joint Committee. In this context, it could be interesting to see how the Court of Justice would interpret the FMA in this respect, in a situation where a national court of an EU Member State requests an advisory opinion based on a case of refusal to reimburse medical treatment for a patient seeking treatment in Switzerland without prior authorisation. Moreover, it is also of great interest to consider whether Switzerland would even wish to incorporate the future Directive on patient rights, which is based on this case law, when it is the Swiss view is that the case law is going beyond the scope of the Agreement.

In relation to Switzerland, it is worth taking a separate look at the *Decker* case which is based on Article 28 EC, namely on the free movement of goods. This freedom is not part of the FMA, but a Free Trade Agreement (FTA) has existed between the EEC and Switzerland since 1972, which contains in Article 13 an identical provision to Article 28 EC.[73] This Agreement has to be purely interpreted in the light of Article 31 of the Vienna Convention on the Law of Treaties. The problem in this respect is that the Court of Justice sees the provisions of free trade agreements generally as directly applicable, while the Swiss Federal Court with regard to Switzerland does not. However, in two judgments from 2005, the Swiss Federal Court was no longer so straight forward in this regard which could be interpreted as an indication of a change in position.[74]

In its second judgment of 8 March 2005 concerning customs duties on imports and exports and charges having equivalent effect (Article 18 and 20 FTA), the Court held that the case law of the Court of Justice based on Article 25 EC is

---

71 OJ L 114 of 10 April 2002, 64. In a second round of bilateral negotiations (*'Bilateral II'*), services were initially part of these negotiations. However, due to problems of Switzerland in adopting fundamental aspects of the *acquis communautaire*, this subject was withdrawn from the negotiations on the request of Switzerland, and has so far not been taken up again.

72 Swiss Federal Court, Case 8C_192/2007, cited above, point 4.3.3–4.3.7; Case I 601/06, cited above, point 6.6, and Case 9C_479/2008, cited above, point 6.2.

73 Free Trade Agreement between the European Economic Community and the Swiss Confederation of 22 July 1972, OJ L 300 of 31 December 1972, 189.

74 See, in particular with regard to judgment of the Swiss Federal Court in case BGE 131 II 295, TOBLER, Christa, *Cassis de Dijon für die Schweiz: pur or on the rocks*, 567.

"*not irrelevant*".[75] This statement is of importance where a provision in national legislation is open to an interpretation based on the Free Trade Agreement. Such a shift in view might have been triggered by the increased proximity of Switzerland via its Agreements concluded in 1999 ('*Bilateral I*') and 2004 ('*Bilateral II*')[76], and many technical agreements that exist between the EU and Switzerland.[77]

Thus, there might be a possibility that the interpretation of national legislation in view of Article 13 FTA in conjunction with the *Decker* case could entail the reimbursement of costs by the Swiss health care system of medicinal products which were acquired outside of Switzerland.

3.3.5. The Concept of European Citizenship Under the FMA

There is no equivalent provision to the concept of European Citizenship in the FMA. As for the question of the interpretation of the FMA *acquis* in the light of citizenship rights, the Swiss Federal Court has mentioned the concept in several cases.

In a judgment of 19 December 2003 concerning residence rights, the Swiss Federal Court held that the FMA does not cover the complete framework of the Internal Market, but only one sector. The judgments of the Court of Justice going beyond this frame could therefore not be applied in the Swiss legal order without any further examination, *i.e.* without a decision by the Joint Committee. It continued stating that "*... the findings of the Court of Justice based on the concept of European Citizenship have to be applied with caution by the Swiss judges... even if they concern the free movement of workers*".[78] It seemed at the time that the Swiss Federal Court did not exclude a restricted application of case law based on citizenship rights.

In a judgment from 2007 again on residence rights, the Federal Court was already much clearer on the subject. It concluded that "*... this concept should not be applied*

75 Swiss Federal Court, Case 1A.71/2004 (BGE 131 II 271)(DE), judgment of 8 March 2005, point 10.3.

76 A second round of bilateral negotiations concerned the association of Switzerland to the Schengen *acquis*, the participation in the Dublin Convention, the European Environment Agency and the European Environment Information and Observation Network, the Media Programme, a statistical co-operation, a Swiss contribution to combat tax fraud and the taxation of savings and measures to avoid double taxation of EU civil servants. The agreements of the *Bilateral II* package were signed in October 2004.

77 IMHOF, E., *Das Freizügigkeitsabkommen EG – Schweiz und seine Auslegungsmethode*, Teil 2, ZESAR 5–6/07, 225.

78 Swiss Federal Court, Case 2A.246/2003 (BGE 130 II 113)(DE), judgment of 19 December 2003, point 6.3.

in relation to Switzerland".[79] This unconditional refusal of the concept is probably related to the dynamic development which the Court of Justice attributed to citizenship rights after 2003.[80]

4. THE EFTA CONVENTION

For sake of completeness, the EFTA Convention concerning bilateral relations between Iceland, Liechtenstein and Norway on the one hand, and Switzerland on the other, should briefly be mentioned.

Like the other two Agreements, it is based on the same structure with a text and Annexes which refer to secondary legislation. The EFTA Council manages the relations between the EFTA States under the EFTA Convention and is the forum in which the EFTA States consult, negotiate and act together. A number of sub-committees manage the updating of the EFTA Convention.

With respect to the social security co-ordination *acquis,* Article 21 of the EFTA Convention is the core provision referring to Annex K, Appendix II, to the Convention, which contains a reference to the incorporated acts in Section A. Article 1 of Appendix II defines the scope of the *acquis* being the Community Acts for social security co-ordination as incorporated in the EEA Agreement and the EC-Swiss Agreement on the free movement of persons, as of 21 June 1999, as amended by Section A of Appendix II. The EFTA Convention contains therefore the smallest common denominator *acquis* of the two prior discussed Agreements.

The *acquis* is consequently equal to the content of the bilateral EC-Swiss Agreement including the same legal questions. I will refrain from restating the issues illustrated above. Suffice it to say that the EFTA Convention is usually the last of the Agreements to be amended since, prior to any amendment, the new legislation in question has to be incorporated into the EEA Agreement and the EU-Swiss Agreement. Therefore, the EFTA Convention currently contains the EU *acquis* of 2004.

---

79 Swiss Federal Court, Case H 31/06 (BGE 133 V 329)(FR), judgment of 4 July 2007, point 8.4.

80 See, in particular, Case C-138/02 *Collins* [2004] ECR I-2703; Case 148/02 *Garcia Avello* [2003] I-11613; Case C-456/02 *Trojani* [2004] ECR I-7573 and Case 200/02 *Zhu and Chen* [2004] ECR I-9925; See also, HALTERN, U., *Europarecht*, 495, and REICH, N., *Understanding EU Law*, 70.

5. SUMMARY AND CONCLUSION

The analysis above illustrates the differences in social security co-ordination based on international agreements concluded by the EC and its Member States in relation to the EFTA States. First of all, the scope of the agreements, the full Internal Market approach of the EEA Agreement, and the sectoral approach of the FMA set out the framework for interpretation of the social security *acquis*. The consequences were illustrated with the examples of reimbursement of cross-border medical treatment based on the principles of service provision and the application of the concept of European citizenship.

The dynamic character of the EEA Agreement and the static character of the FMA lead to disparities in the development of the Agreements. Differences in the social security *acquis* are linked to a time element, as the frequency and regularity of amendments of the different types of Agreements vary tremendously. In this respect, the impact of new case law of the Court of Justice was demonstrated with the development of special non-contributory benefits.

Finally, it is also important to underline that the personal scope of the Agreements is restricted to nationals of the contracting parties. The integration element of third country nationals is very limited in those agreements. EC secondary legislation specifically addressing third parties is not part of the Agreements. This might result in lack of legal certainty for the migrating persons or even lead to gaps in the social security coverage as illustrated with the example of third country nationals using their EHIC in the EFTA States.

LITERATURE

BAUDENBACHER, Carl, *Facets of an EEA constitutional order*, in COLNERIC et al. (ed.), *Une Communauté de droit*, Festschrift für Gil Carlos Rodrígues Iglesias, BWV, 2004, 343

BAUDENBACHER, Carl, *The EFTA Court: an actor in the European judicial dialogue*, Fordham International Law Journal, Vol. 28, 2005, 353

BAUDENBACHER, Carl, *Governments before the EFTA Court*, in Festskrift til Claus Gulmann, forlaget Thomson, Copenhagen, 2006, 23

BAUDENBACHER, Carl, *The contribution of the EFTA Court to the establishment of a homogeneous and dynamic European Economic Area*, at the occasion of the biannual EFTA Seminar on 12/13 June 2008

BAUDENBACHER, Carl, *Der EFTA Gerichtshof, das EWR-Abkommen und die Fortentwicklungen des EG-Vertrags*, in Festschrift zum 75. Geburtstag von Prof. Dr. Dr. Herbert Batliner, 63

BREMER, Frank, *Liechtenstein's helplessness allowance: the EFTA Court quashes residence requirement*, European Law Reporter 7–8, 2008, 261

FENGER, Niels, *Limits to a Dynamic Homogeneity between EC Law and EEA Law*, in Festskrift til Claus Gulmann, forlaget Thomson, Copenhagen 2006, 144

FENGER/SANCHEZ/VAN STIPHOUT, in BLANPAIN/WOUTERS (eds.) International Encyclopaedia of Laws, Intergovernmental Organisations, Supplement 24, European Free Trade Association (EFTA) and European Economic Area (EEA), Kluwer Law International, 2005, 1

FORMAN, John, *The EEA Agreement five years on: Dynamic homogeneity in practise and its implementation by the two EEA Courts*, Common Market Law Review 36, 1999, 751–781

GRAVER, Hans Petter, *The EFTA Court and the Court of Justice of the EC: Legal homogeneity at stake?*, in MÜLLER-GRAFF/SELVIG (eds.), *EEA-EU relations*, Berlin: Berlin Verlag, 1999, 31

GRAVER, Hans Petter, *Mission impossible: supranationality and national legal autonomy in the EEA Agreement*, European Foreign Affairs Review 7, 2002, 73

HALTERN, Ulrich, *Europarecht*, Mohr Siebeck, Tübingen, 2005

IMHOF, Edgar, *Das Freizügigkeitsabkommen EG - Schweiz und seine Auslegungsmethode*, Teil 1, ZESAR 4/07, 155

IMHOF, Edgar, *Das Freizügigkeitsabkommen EG – Schweiz und seine Auslegungsmethode*, Teil 2, ZESAR 5–6/07, 220

ÖRLYGSSON, Thorgeir, *Iceland and the EFTA Court*, in Festschrift for Carl Baudenbacher, *Economic Law and Justice in Times of Globalisation*, Nomos, Baden-Baden 2007, 225

REICH, Norbert, *Understanding EU Law*, 2nd edition, Intersentia, 2005

SEVON, Leif, *Primacy and Direct Effect in the EEA. Some Reflections*, in Festskrift til Ole Due, GEG Gode Forlag, Kobenhavn, 1994, 340

TOBLER, Christa, *Cassis de Dijon für die Schweiz: pur or on the rocks*, in Schweizerische Zeitschrift für internationales und europäisches Recht (SZIER), Zürich, 4/2005, 567

VAN GERVEN, Walter, *The genesis of EEA law and principles of primacy and direct effect*, in Fordham International Law Journal, Vol. 16, 1992–1993, 955

ANNEX: THE TWO-PILLAR STRUCTURE UNDER THE EEA AGREEMENT

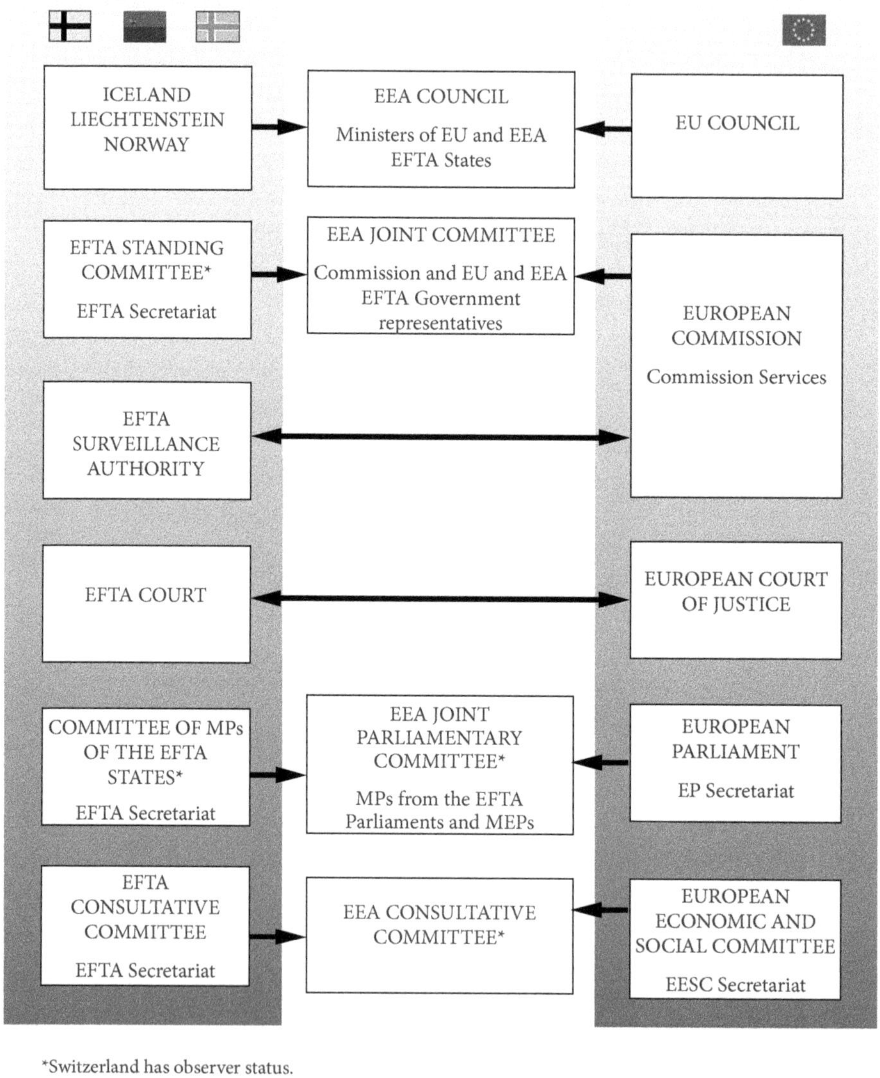

Source: X, *This is EFTA. 2009*, Brussels, 2009.

THE EXISTING BILATERAL AND MULTILATERAL SOCIAL SECURITY INSTRUMENTS BINDING EU STATES AND NON-EU STATES

GREGA STRBAN*

1. INTRODUCTORY REMARKS

International social security law is an intrinsic part of international law. Legal norms of international social security law are as a rule agreed upon between the States as primary and most important subjects of international law.[1]

According to their *origin* they may be enshrined in agreements only between two States, i.e. bilateral agreements (of substantive or administrative nature, in one instrument or as exchange of notes etc.), or in agreements between three or more States, i.e. multilateral agreements (covenants, conventions, charters, protocols etc.).

Due to distinctive titles of legal acts containing norms of international social security law, the notion of *international social security instruments* will be used. Their common characteristics are written form and common will of the contracting parties, who accept obligations and determine certain rights. The latter may also be agreed to the benefit of third parties, i.e. individual persons.

International social security instruments may be concluded with a distinctive *purpose* and thus contain norms of distinctive legal character. They might tend to harmonise various national social security systems, by introducing e.g. minimum standards. On the other hand they might be linking or coordinating various social security systems in order for migrating persons not to loose their social security entitlements.[2] Only the latter will be dealt with in this paper.[3]

---

* Prof. Grega Strban is professor at the Faculty of Law of the University of Ljubljana. This text was written in spring 2009.

1 *Türk*, 2007, p. 19.

2 *Pieters*, 2006, p. 125.

3 Other distinctions are possible as well, for instance according to the scope of application (universal or regional), legal nature (legally binding or non-binding) etc.

One of the *broadest definitions* of international social security law encompasses all social security norms regulating matters with international element.[4] Hence, not only international, but also supranational and even national collision or substantive norms exceeding the boundaries of only one State are taken into account.[5]

In this paper social security *supranational law*, i.e. the law of the European Community (EC) will not be analysed as such. The EC social security co-ordination regulations are beyond any doubt the most important social security co-ordination instruments in Europe. They are being constantly developed by the legislator and especially by the Court of Justice of the European Communities (ECJ), making them probably the most comprehensive and complex social security co-ordination legal instruments in the world. Yet, it would be wrong to believe that there are no other bilateral and multilateral social security co-ordination instruments which bear interest also for the European Union (EU) Member States, when people move to or form a country outside the EU.

Social security co-ordination, achieved with *unilateral measures* of a single State, will also be left aside in this paper. It should suffice to note that the restrictions of territorial or nationality nature might be mastered with national substantive (e.g. making no distinction on the grounds of nationality) or collision norms. They may regulate situations of national law producing effects in other States, e.g. unrestricted export of benefits, and taking into account legal norms of other States, e.g. by restricting the applicability of national law in case of entitlements from other States. In addition to the legislator, the judiciary might play an important role in applying not only international, but also solely national norms.[6]

Nationality requirements, territorial restrictions (e.g. counting only periods of insurance or residence completed on the territory of a respected State, not exporting benefits etc.), might to a certain extent be alleviated by national legislative efforts, encouraged also by certain international instruments.[7] However, at the end the realisation of effective solutions requires linking together of national social security systems on the grounds of international social security instruments.

4 *Steinmeyer*, 2003, p. 31.

5 *Eichenhofer*, 1994, p. 2 ff.

6 For instance, the German Federal Constitutional Court in 1979 declared export restrictions for pensions incompatible with the constitutional protection of property. *Vonk*, 2002, p. 86. Slovenian Constitutional Court (U-I-31/04, 1 December 2005) declared permanent residence of the child (as a condition for a child benefit) incompatible with the constitutional principle of equality.

7 For instance, Paragraph 4 of Article 12 of the (initial and revised) European Social Charter.

2. BILATERAL AGREEMENTS BINDING EU AND NON-EU STATES

The boundaries of this paper would be exceeded, if all the existing bilateral agreements between EU and non-EU States in the world would be analysed in great detail. Nevertheless, it is important to note that not all bilateral agreements are equal in their material and personal scope of application. It is therefore required to present the evolution and main features of the existing bilateral agreements binding EU and non-EU states.

2.1. THE EVOLUTION

Social security bilateral agreements were historically the first international instruments to co-ordinate national social security systems. Their intention was to ensure decent protection for persons travelling or residing abroad.

This concern first appeared at the beginning of the 19th century. The first social security bilateral agreement was concluded between France and the Dukedom of Parma on the 13th of August 1827. It has guaranteed the payment of pensions from one State to nationals of the other State according to the principle of reciprocity and without the conditions of residence on the territory of the State providing the pension.[8]

This, historically first period of international social security law lasted from 1827 until the 15th of April 1904, when the bilateral agreement between France and Italy on social insurance application and worker's protection for nationals of both contracting States was concluded.[9] This period is classified by some authors as *pre-history of international social security law.*[10] With the exception of 1827 agreement, only bilateral agreements on social assistance for certain groups of persons in need were concluded in this period.[11]

Their purpose was to recognise and apply the principle of equal treatment in social assistance. Emphasis of this fundamental social security co-ordination principle can be reasonably explained. Statutory social protection was limited to social assistance and it was required to provide it also to foreigners in need. However, legal reciprocity was essential element of these relations, since social

8 *Perrin*, 1983, p. 3.
9 Sometimes this agreement is mentioned as the first bilateral social security agreement. *Vonk*, 2002, p. 79.
10 *Perrin*, 1983, p. 4.
11 The agreement between Bavaria and Saxony from 1833 is mentioned as the first one. *Ibidem.*

assistance was limited to national territory and was a burden of local community. With bilateral agreement and reciprocity requirement a contracting State solved the problem of its nationals requiring assistance outside of its territory.[12]

Bilateral social security agreement from 1904 introduced a new phase of bilateral agreements. Conclusion of many other social security agreements intensified. Until the First World War they concerned mainly equality of treatment in social insurance and co-ordination in case of compensation for accidents at work and occupational diseases, also between current EU and non-EU States.[13] These agreements were a step forward, especially concerning the determination of the applicable legislation and administrative assistance.

Many more bilateral agreements were concluded after the Second World War. Even today bilateral social security agreements are the most important source of social security co-ordination, at least for the States, who are not Members of the EU and have ratified no or only few multilateral social security instruments.

2.2. EXISTING BILATERAL SOCIAL SECURITY AGREEMENTS

Bilateral social security agreements tend to reflect migration patterns (which relate to geography, language, culture)[14] and more or less restrictive immigration policies[15] towards some countries and in certain time period. Hence, in practice they vary to a great extent and are tailored to specific social security systems of the contracting parties.

Even if they are *complete* agreements, i.e. encompassing all social security co-ordination principles[16], or covering all social insurance branches[17] distinctive formulations and features may be applied. However, their common characteristics are written form, unlimited duration (open-ended agreements) and reliance on the principle of reciprocity.

---

12 *Ibidem*, p. 7.

13 For instance, the agreement between Italy and Switzerland (1904). *Ibidem*, p. 27.

14 *Nickless/Siedl*, 2004, p. 14.

15 *Vonk*, 2002, p. 82.

16 They contain norms on equality of treatment of nationals of both contracting States, the applicable legislation, protection of rights in course of acquisition and acquired rights, and administrative and legal assistance. *Petersen*, 2003, p. 1702.

17 *Schulte*, 1995, p. 130.

2.2.1. *Material Scope of Application*

Bilateral social security agreements between EU and non-EU States are rarely concluded in the field of social assistance.[18] Normally, they regulate co-ordination related to traditional social risks, contained also in the ILO Convention No. 102, sometimes explicitly excluding social assistance and new social insurance branches.[19] In continental Europe traditional social risks are covered by social insurances. Hence, certain bilateral agreements mention social insurance already in their title[20], while others speak about social security[21], but sometimes without much distinction.

Some, especially older bilateral agreements, define the legislation for which the agreement should apply *ratione materiae*.[22] In contemporary bilateral agreements, only social insurance branches are usually mentioned, and not the legislation regulating them.[23] Such normative technique enables the applicability of the bilateral agreement also to new legislative acts in a specific field of social security law, often considered to be one of the most rapidly changing areas of law.

However, also bilateral agreements concluded with other (third) States are part of legislation in a specific social insurance field. In order to avoid such interpretation some bilateral social security agreements stipulate that other agreements will not be taken into account when applying specific bilateral agreement between the contracting parties.[24] Yet others stipulate that agreements with third parties will be taken into account, e.g. in the field of pensions.[25]

Complete or comprehensive bilateral agreements may cover not only pension, invalidity, survivors and health insurance, accidents at work and occupational diseases schemes, but also unemployment and family benefits.[26] Others might be restricted to certain social insurance branches[27] or only one branch, e.g. pension

18 For instance, bilateral agreement between Germany and Switzerland (1952). *Petersen*, 2003, p. 1707.

19 For instance, the agreement between the Netherlands and Croatia (1998).

20 For instance, the agreement on social insurance between Slovenia and Croatia (1997).

21 For instance, agreements Slovenia concluded with Argentina (2007), Australia (2002), Canada and Quebec (1998, 2000).

22 For instance, the agreement between United Kingdom and former Yugoslavia from 1958 (on UK's side, but with a note that subsequent amendments should be taken into account).

23 Normally material scope is defined in the Article 2 of each bilateral agreement.

24 Such stipulation could be found in agreements concluded by Germany. *Petersen*, 2003, p. 1709.

25 For instance, the agreement between Czech Republic and Croatia (1999).

26 For instance, bilateral agreements between Belgium and Croatia (2001), Slovenia and Bosnia and Herzegovina (2007).

27 For instance, the agreement between Germany and Croatia (1997) is limited to health, pension and invalidity insurance.

insurance. The later is due to the fact that for long term benefits longer insurance periods are required, which can be build also in more remote countries.[28]

2.2.2. Personal Scope of Application

Some bilateral social security agreements are limited only to nationals of both contracting States. They are defined as *closed* bilateral agreements. However, they may be applicable also to refuges and stateless persons. Their scope *ratione personae* may also be extended to family members who enjoy derived rights from an insured person, even if they themselves are not nationals of one of the contracting States.[29]

Closed personal scope is a characteristic of some older bilateral agreements.[30] Nevertheless, it might still be found in some newer bilateral agreements concluded between EU and non-EU States.[31]

On the other hand, bilateral agreements which are not limited only to nationals of the contracting States are defined as *open* or *universally applicable* agreements. Usually they apply to all persons covered by the social security legislation of one or both contracting parties and persons enjoying derived rights. These agreements were mainly concluded between EU and non-EU States in more recent time.[32]

Open agreements are open in their personal scope and in application of general principles of social security co-ordination. For instance, in such agreements the principle of equal treatment applies to all persons covered under the agreement.[33]

However, and now it becomes interesting, some open agreements, i.e. covering all insured persons, whatever their nationality, restrict the application of equality

28 For instance, Pension insurance agreement between Germany and Chile (1993), the agreement between Slovenia and Australia (2002).

29 *Petersen*, 2003, p. 1710.

30 For instance, bilateral agreements Germany concluded with Morocco (1981), and Tunisia (1984), or agreements concluded by former Yugoslavia with France (1950) Sweden (1978), United Kingdom (1958). The later agreements are still applied for certain former Yugoslav Republics, now independent States.

31 For instance, agreements Croatia concluded with Denmark (2005), Italy (1997), or Bulgaria (2003).

32 For instance, agreements Germany concluded with Australia (2000), and Japan (1998), Slovenia with Croatia (1997), Canada and Quebec (1998, 2000), Australia (2002), Macedonia (1998), Bosnia and Herzegovina (2007), the Netherlands with Croatia (1998), Austria with Croatia (1997) etc.

33 For instance Articles 4 of bilateral agreements Slovenia concluded with Australia (2002), Canada and Quebec (1998, 2000).

principle only to nationals of the contracting States.[34] Hence, open agreements are not completely universally applicable after all. They still contain some reminiscence of nationality condition.

2.2.3. Equality of Treatment

Next to equality of treatment of all persons covered by the bilateral agreement or just nationals of the contracting states, some agreements may extend this principle to nationals of third countries (not just family members). For instance, EU nationals may be treated equally as nationals of a contracting party.[35]

Such provision is a reflection of the ECJ's rulings, especially in the leading case *Gottardo*.[36] ECJ established that when an EU Member State concludes a bilateral agreement with a non-Member State, the fundamental principle of equal treatment requires that Member State to grant nationals of other EU Member States the same advantages as those which its own nationals enjoy under that agreement. While applying bilateral agreements Member States are still bound by the EC law in relation to each other. They are required to comply with the obligations that Community law imposes on them, especially under Articles 12 and 39 EC Treaty.

Exception is possible only, if objective justification is provided. The Court found that increased financial burden and administrative difficulties cannot constitute an objective justification. Disturbing the balance and reciprocity of a bilateral agreement, however, may constitute such justification. Additionally, such extension of a bilateral agreement should neither compromise the rights non-EU State derives from the agreement nor impose any new obligations on that State. The latter is under no obligation to comply with the EC law.

An interesting question may concern third country nationals. Could they also enjoy the advantages of the *Gottardo* principle, for instance when moving between two EU Member States and a non-EU State? Some seem to argue in the affirmative.[37] Also the Court argued that when giving effect to commitments assumed under bilateral agreements, be it an agreement between EU Member States *or an agreement between a Member State and a non-Member State*, Member States are required to comply with the obligations that Community law imposes on them.

---

34 For instance, the agreement between the Netherlands and Croatia (1998, Article 4), agreements Slovenia concluded with Croatia (1997), Macedonia (1998), Bosnia and Herzegovina (2007), the agreement between Austria and Croatia (1997).

35 For instance, Article 4 of the agreement between Hungary and Croatia (2005).

36 *Gottardo*, C-55/00, ECR 2002, p. I-413.

37 *Vonk*, 2006, p. 18.

And in the EC social security co-ordination law third country nationals have to be treated equally as EU nationals.[38]

Additionally, some bilateral agreements provide for co called assimilation of facts and events occurred on the territory of a contracting party.[39]

2.2.4. Determining the Applicable Legislation

Bilateral social security agreements may be based on the principle of integration (called also principle of incorporation or principle of territoriality) or the principle of insurance. According the *principle of integration*, social security benefits should be provided by the contracting State or insurance carrier on which territory social risk materialised. For instance, pensions should be calculated and provided only in the residence State, taking into account also relevant periods completed in the other contracting State.

Similar rules apply to medical benefits. They should be provided in the State of residence regardless of the fact that person might be covered by mandatory health insurance in another State.

As such, nothing is wrong with this, rather straight forward co-ordination principle. However, problems might arise with income-related benefits, and rather short periods of residence in the State.[40] It could be argued that it would make sense, if balance would be achieved in international labour distribution. Until then it could be used between the States with equal or similar migration patterns and comparably advanced social security systems.

According to the *principle of insurance* the contracting State where a worker or other person performs economic activity is responsible for collecting contributions and providing benefits. Applicable legislation is thus the legislation of the State where economic activity is performed (*lex loci laboris*). Insurance of one State is extended also to the territory of another State. For instance, pensions will be provided by each of the States where person has been insured, and medical benefits will be paid by the insurance carrier, even if they are provided in the State of residence.[41]

---

38 C.f. also previous case law of the ECJ, e.g. *Grana Novoa* (C-23/92, ECR 1993, p. I-4505). The Court held that a bilateral agreement between a single EU Member State and non-EU State does not come within the concept of legislation, as that term is used in regulation 1408/71.

39 For instance, the bilateral agreement between Germany and Chile (1993). *Petersen*, 2003, p. 1713. Articles 6 of agreements Slovenia concluded with Macedonia (1998), Croatia (1997), Bosnia and Herzegovina (2007).

40 It may lead to unacceptable and unjust results when paying long-term benefits. *Pennings*, 2003, p. 179.

41 *Rismondo*, 2007, p. 5.

Exceptions to the *lex loci laboris* rule are possible. They apply for example to posted workers, workers in international transport, seamen, civil servants, diplomats etc. They normally remain insured in their State of origin. In some cases exemption on demand of employer and worker, with consent of representatives of both States is also possible.[42] This is an example of so called flexibility clause, used also to prolong posting periods.

Some of the older bilateral agreements are characterised by the integration method, whereas new ones are as a rule based on the principle of insurance.[43] However, also the latter may contain provisions expressing the principle of territoriality. For instance, medical benefits may be provided by and on the account of the insurance carrier in the State of residence for persons receiving pensions from both contracting States.[44] Similar rules may apply in case of accident at work or occupational disease.[45]

2.2.5. Protection of Rights in Course of Acquisition

Aggregation or *totalisation* of all relevant periods (insurance, employment or residence) is the main technique to protect legal expectations. According to bilateral agreements this rule is used only, if insurance period completed in one contracting State would not suffice to guarantee access to a certain right. Only then period of insurance in the other contracting state is taken into account and *pro-rata temporis* pension calculated.[46] Normally, the periods should not overlap. Aggregation rule is applied to all social security benefits, conditioned with prior insurance period.[47]

Interestingly enough, more modern agreements are not restricted only to the relevant periods completed in both contracting states, but may extend also to periods from third States. A condition may be that both contracting States have concluded separate bilateral agreements with the third country. If only one has

42 For instance, agreements between Austria and Croatia (1997, Article 9), Slovenia and Bosnia and Herzegovina (2007, Article 10).

43 For instance, Articles 7 of bilateral agreements between Slovenia and Bosnia and Herzegovina (2007), the Netherlands and Croatia (1998), Denmark and Croatia (2005).

44 For instance, agreements between Belgium and Croatia (2005, Article 16), the Netherlands and Croatia (1998, Article 19).

45 For instance, if a person was employed in both States, on working places which could lead to occupational disease, the State of last employment is solely responsible for benefits to the victim or his/her survivors. For instance, agreements between Belgium and Croatia (2005, Article 23), Slovenia and Croatia (1997, Article 21).

46 For instance, Article 16 of the agreement between Bulgaria and Croatia (2003).

47 For instance, for unemployment benefits in agreements between Belgium and Croatia (2005, Article 36), Slovenia and Macedonia (1998, Article 25), for health insurance benefits in the agreement between Slovenia and Bosnia and Herzegovina (2007, Article 11).

done so, this kind of third country clause might be applicable only to persons (nationals or all persons) covered by the agreement with the third country.[48]

In some agreements with non-EU States, the reflection of the so called *Petroni* principle[49] (principle of *favourability*)[50] may be found on the side of EU States. For instance, Belgian insurance carrier has to calculate two amounts of a pension. If possible, one should be on the ground of Belgian legislation alone, and the other on the ground of theoretical amount and the *pro-rata-temporis* pension. The higher of both should actually be paid.[51]

2.2.6. Protection of Acquired Rights

Vested rights are as a rule protected with export of benefits. However, not all benefits are being exported to the same extent. For instance, export of benefits in kind, most notably medical benefits, is restricted. They may be provided in the other contracting State in case of established residence there, prior authorisation or urgent medical treatment.[52] In some agreements also the term utmost urgent medical treatment is used.[53] The term necessary medical treatment, as in the EC social security co-ordination law, is rarely applied. It could be argued, that whatever the term used, it is always the decision of a certain physician that fills the term in a concrete case.

Cash benefits are as a rule exported to the territory of the contracting party. Some agreements define this as an equalisation of territories.[54] Exceptions have to be expressly agreed.

Some modern bilateral agreements between EU and non-EU States go a step further. Benefits are to be provided to the contracting State's nationals, even if they reside in a third country, under the same conditions as to their own nationals.[55] This is a so called *national treatment of non-nationals*.[56] Hence, if

---

48 For instance, agreements between Belgium and Croatia (2001, Article 26), the Netherlands and Croatia (Article 21), agreements Slovenia concluded with Macedonia (1998, Article 21), Croatia (1997, Article 22), Bosnia and Herzegovina (2007, Article 20).

49 After the ECJ's decision in case *Petroni* (C-24/75, ECR 1975, p. 1149).

50 *Schoukens*, 2004–2005, p. 30.

51 For instance, the agreement between Belgium and Croatia (2001, Articles 26).

52 For instance, agreements between Austria and Croatia (1997, Article 11), Slovenia and Bosnia and Herzegovina (2007, Article 12).

53 For instance, the agreement between Belgium and Croatia (2001, Article 13).

54 For instance, marginal title to Article 5 of the agreement between Hungary and Croatia (2005).

55 For instance Articles 5 of the bilateral agreement between Belgium and Croatia (2001), agreements Slovenia concluded with Macedonia (1998), Bosnia and Herzegovina (2007).

56 *Schulte*, 1995, p. 132.

benefits provided to nationals of a contracting State are exported, either on the grounds of national law alone or on the grounds of bilateral agreement with a third country, they should also be exported for the nationals of the other contracting State.

2.2.7. Principle of Good Administration

This, so called fifth principle, which comes more to the forefront in the new EC social security co-ordination law, is also enshrined in modern bilateral social security agreements. Effective execution of an agreement and provision of social security benefits in a concrete cross-border case is not possible without an excellent administrative and legal cooperation between the responsible institutions of the contracting States.

It is essential, for instance to share information on the nature and duration of insurance period completed in each of the social security systems, exchange forms etc. Due to limits presented by the territoriality principle, national legislator cannot extend the duty to administrative and legal cooperation to administrative bodies, social security carriers and courts in another country. Hence, specific provisions, contained in bilateral agreements are required.[57]

Some newer bilateral agreements usually emphasise the duty to share information, administrative and legal assistance free of charge, possibility of lodging claims in other than official language, with the institution where the claimant resides, recognition of decisions, alternative dispute resolution procedure etc.[58] Some contain special provisions on data protection.[59] Usually, special administrative agreements are concluded to implement the bilateral social security agreement.[60]

2.3. PROMOTION OF BILATERAL AGREEMENTS

Both, the International Labour organisation (ILO) and the Council of Europe (CoE) *consider bilateral agreements as good practice and promote their conclusion.* ILO has already in 1949[61] inserted a *Model Agreement on Temporary and Permanent Migration for Employment, including Migration of Refugees and Displaced Persons* in Annex of the Recommendation No. 86 on Migration for Employment.

57 *Petersen*, 2003, p. 1721.
58 For instance, Article 27 and following of the agreement between Slovenia and Macedonia (1998).
59 For instance, Article 35 of the agreement between Germany and Croatia (1997).
60 For instance, administrative agreements between Belgium in Croatia (2002), Slovenia and Macedonia (1998).
61 ILO's first model provisions seem to be issued already in 1928. *Rismondo*, 2007, p. 6.

Article 21 of the Model Agreement is concerned with social security. It envisages a conclusion of a separate social security bilateral agreement, which should encompass basic principles of social security co-ordination. Hence, migrant workers and their dependants should not be treated less favourably then nationals of the State, and their rights in course of acquisition and acquired right should be protected.[62]

In 1983 the ILO issued more specific model provisions. *Model Agreement for the co-ordination of bilateral or multilateral social security instruments* was included in the Annex II of the Recommendation No. 167 on Maintenance of Social Security Rights. This Recommendation is linked to the Convention No. 157.

Also in the CoE there is a great emphasis on social security model provisions. The *European Convention on Social Security* consists partially of model provisions. Additionally, *Model Provisions for a Bilateral Social Security Agreement* (1998) should assist the CoE Member States, in particular those from Central and Eastern Europe (having joined the CoE recently) with the drawing up of bilateral agreements on social security. They are available not only in English and French, but also in Albanian, Macedonian, Romanian and Serbian language.[63]

Model provisions for a Bilateral Social Security Agreement are a flexible instrument and incorporate all basic principles of social security co-ordination. They are divided into five parts, covering general provisions, determining the applicable legislation, specific provisions of each of the social security branches, miscellaneous provisions, transitional and final provisions. Model provisions respect the differences in social security arrangements and provide alternative suggestions wherever possible. Additionally, they are supported by an explanatory report, which aims to make suggested provisions easier to understand.[64]

All model provisions are of a *non-binding legal nature.* They purpose is to act as a guide to the States that wish to conclude a bilateral social security agreement. The States are free to alter their content, determine the range of persons and benefits to be covered.

Despite the promotion of bilateral agreements, a decade ago they were hardly any bilateral agreements between EU Member States and States in certain regions of the World. For instance, very few agreements were in place with Sub-Saharan African States (with the exception of agreement between France and Senegal), Indian subcontinent States (with the exception of agreement between Denmark

62 The regard should also bet taken to the principles of the 1935 Maintenance of Migrants' Pension Rights Convention, or of any revision of that Convention.
63 Accessible at www.coe.int.
64 Model provisions are explained in detail in *Nickless/Siedl*, 2004. pp. 73–87.

and Pakistan), other Asian countries (with the exception of agreements Philippines concluded with Italy and Spain). The reason seems to be that these are mainly emigration countries, and the reciprocity condition, a cornerstone of any bilateral agreement, is lacking.[65]

In recent years the situation seems to be improving. For instance, Belgium has concluded a bilateral social security agreements with Japan (2005) and India (2006, it should come into effect in June 2009).[66] India has also signed bilateral social security agreements with France (2008) and Germany (2008, only for posted workers).[67] The latter concluded bilateral agreements with Japan (1998), Korea (2000) and China (2002, only for posted workers).[68]

3. MULTILATERAL INSTRUMENTS BINDING EU AND NON-EU STATES

Sometimes, when issues concerning more than two states (i.e. multilateral issues) arise, they cannot effectively be dealt with in a bilateral way. Also various third country clauses in bilateral agreements (discussed supra) send a clear signal for the need of multilateral approach.

Multilateral instruments can be agreed upon either between several States directly or within international organisations. They may be instruments primarily dealing with social security co-ordination, but not necessarily. Multilateral instruments, which bear some importance for social security co-ordination, may primarily concern social security harmonisation, legal position of migrant workers, or human rights as such.

3.1. MULTILATERAL INSTRUMENTS AGREED UPON BY THE STATES DIRECTLY

It seems that the first multilateral instrument was agreed upon already in 1919. The *Declaration concerning the compensation for industrial accidents* was concluded between the Nordic States.[69]

---

65 More *Roberts*, 2000, p. 8.

66 Agreement between Belgium and India is a modern, open agreement, applicable to all insured persons, to whom the equal treatment principle should apply (it is not restricted to nationals, Articles 3 and 4).

67 India seems to have completed negotiations for a bilateral social security agreement with Czech Republic, the Netherlands, Luxembourg, and negotiations seem to be underway with Sweden and Hungary.

68 *BMAS*, 2009.

69 *Perrin*, 1983, p. 28.

The example of an existing multilateral social security co-ordination agreement, concluded by the States directly, might be the *Nordic Convention on Social Security* (1955, subsequently revised). It is concluded between EU States (Denmark, Finland, Sweden) and non-EU States (Iceland, Norway). True, the EC social security co-ordination Regulations apply to all this States, EU and EEA Members. However, it could be argued, that Nordic Convention is broader in scope, covering also all non active persons.[70]

Another example might be the *Ibero-American Multilateral Convention of Social Security* (2007) concluded in Chile, by the EU and non-EU States.[71] It is quite a modern, multilateral social security instrument. It is open in its personal scope of application (to all insured persons under the legislation of a contracting State) and in application of the equal treatment principle.[72]

Interestingly, the *EC social security co-ordination Regulations* also evolved from a multilateral agreement, concluded among the six founding States. However, it has subsequently not been implemented as such, but entered into force as an EEC Regulation.[73]

3.2. UNITED NATIONS

The *Universal declaration of Human Rights* (1948) and the *International Covenant on Economic, Social and Cultural Rights* (1966) enshrine the right to social security to everyone. All individuals, irrespective of any personal circumstance (also national origin) are born free and equal in dignity and rights. Everyone as a member of a society has the right to social security and is entitled to its realization, through national effort and international cooperation.[74] Persons migrating or simply moving between countries included.[75]

---

70 E.g. Article 3 of the Nordic Convention, 1993.

71 There are as much as 22 State Parties. They are Portugal, Spain and Andorra on the European side and Argentina, Bolivia, Brasilia, Chile, Colombia, Costa Rica, Cuba, Ecuador, El Salvador (which has as first State ratified the convention in 2008), Guatemala, Honduras, Mexico, Nicaragua, Panama, Paraguay, Peru, Dominican Republic, Uruguay and Venezuela on the Latin America's side.

72 Articles 2 and 4 of the Convention. The full text of the *Convenio Multilateral Iberoamericano de Seguridad Social* is accessible at www.oiss.org.

73 *Shulte*, 1995, p. 132.

74 Articles 22 and 25 of the Universal Declaration of Human Rights, and Article 9 of the International Covenant on Social, Economic and Cultural Rights.

75 Special attention is paid to equality of treatment of migrant workers in the General Comment No. 19 on The right to social security (especially points 36–38) under the International Covenant on Social, Economic and Cultural Rights, issued by the UN Economic and Social

In 1990 the *International Convention on the Protection of the Rights of All Migrant Workers and Members of Their Families* was adopted by the United Nations' (UN) General Assembly. It entered into force on the 1st of July 2003. This convention emphasises only one principle of social security co-ordination, i.e. equality of treatment.[76] Despite 41 ratifications and 15 signatures by the end of March 2009, none of the EU Member States has signed the Convention.[77] Thus, it is of a minor importance for the present research.

3.3. NORMS OF THE INTERNATIONAL LABOUR ORGANISATION

International Labour Organisation is one of the most active international organisations in the field of social security. Several conventions are devoted specifically to social security co-ordination.

3.3.1. ILO Social Security Co-ordination Conventions

Already in 1925 the *Equality of Treatment (Accident Compensation) Convention (No. 19)* was adopted by the International Labour Conference. It is not a comprehensive social security co-ordination instrument. It deals with only one principle, i.e. equality of treatment of nationals (and their dependants) of other contracting States, without any residence condition. Benefits of foreign workers should be exported, if the contracting State provides for such export for its own nationals. To this end, special agreements between States may be concluded, if necessary.[78]

The Convention deals also with only one social security scheme, i.e. compensations for industrial accidents. Separate agreements and mutual assistance are promoted. ILO Convention No. 19 is still applicable[79] and has been widely ratified by EU and non-EU States.[80]

Council in February 2008. Conclusion of international social security co-ordination instruments is advocated (e.g. point 56).

76 Articles 27 and 28 provide for equal treatment of nationals of other contracting states in the field of social security and urgent medical treatment.

77 It was ratified by some (non-EU) European States, e.g. Albania, Bosnia and Herzegovina. The last ratification was by Niger (2009). More info at www.migrantsrights.org.

78 *Kalčič*, in Novak/Končar/Bubnov Škoberne (eds.), 2006, p. 339.

79 According to ILO classification it is an instrument with interim status (hence not outdated, but also not up to date).

80 Until the beginning of March 2009 as much as 121 States have ratified the Convention No. 19, including e.g. Slovenia (successor of former Yugoslavia), Belgium, the Netherlands, France, Germany, Argentina, Brazil, Chile, Peru, China, India etc.

In the 1962 the *Equality of Treatment (Social Security) Convention (No. 118)* the equality of treatment principle has been extended to all nine traditional social security risks, covered by the ILO Convention No. 102. Despite that, the Convention No. 118 has not revised the Convention No. 19.

For each of the nine branches that it accepts, a contracting State undertakes to grant within its territory to nationals of any other contracting State equality of treatment with its own nationals. But it also provides for some flexibility permitting exclusions of non-nationals in case when benefits or parts of benefits are payable out of public funds (e.g. social assistance). Further, contracting States should endeavour to participate in schemes for the maintenance of the acquired rights and rights in course of acquisition.

The Convention No. 118 is considered an up to date instrument, which has been ratified by 37 States, members and non-members of the EU.[81] Interestingly, the Netherlands is the only State which has denounced the Convention. It has done so in 2004, because a national court has recognised its direct applicability. Hence, awarding direct effect to an instrument can also have adverse effects, as States no longer want to be bound by it.[82]

In the 1935 *Maintenance of Migrant's Pension Rights Convention (No. 48)* not only one, but several social security co-ordination principles are enshrined. Rights in course of acquisition and already acquired rights should be protected (with totalisation of relevant periods and export of benefits). Additionally, equality of treatment[83] and mutual administrative assistance should be provided.

However, the material scope of the Convention No. 48 is restricted. It establishes an international multilateral cooperation scheme only in the field of pensions, i.e. old-age, invalidity and survivor's pensions.

Although, the Convention No. 48 is considered to be an outdated instrument, it is still relevant to those States that have not ratified its successor, i.e. the Convention No. 157.[84] And due to low number of ratifications of the latter, the Convention 48 is still applicable for all the ratifying States. Interestingly enough, Convention No. 48 has, after it has been denounced by several States[85], become a more or less

81 Convention No. 118 has been ratified e.g. by France, Germany, India, Jordan, Madagascar, Mexico. It has not been ratified by e.g. Slovenia, Belgium.

82 *Pennings*, in Pennings (ed.), 2007, p. 19.

83 According to Article 18 of the Convention No. 48, each contracting State has to treat nationals of other contracting State on the same footing as its own nationals for the purpose of liability to compulsory insurance and for the purpose of insurance benefits.

84 *Pennings/Shulte*, in Pennings (ed.), 2006, p. 11.

85 It has been denounced by Hungary, the Netherlands, Poland and Spain. On the reasons from the Dutch aspect *Pennings*, in Pennings (ed.), 2006, p. 88.

regional co-ordination instrument. It applies only to the successor States of former Yugoslavia[86], Italy and Israel. Hence, it may be of an utmost importance between EU and non-EU States, between which no bilateral agreement exists, e.g. between Slovenia and Serbia.

The *Maintenance of Social Security Rights Convention, 1982 (No. 157)* has revised the Convention No. 48. It is a comprehensive social security co-ordination instrument, as it covers all nine traditional branches of social security and all co-ordination principles. The Convention is directly applicable in some parts and encourages the conclusion of bilateral or multilateral social security agreements in others (Article 4), covering also non-active persons (Article 5). As already mentioned above, the Recommendation No. 167, accompanying the Convention, contains model provisions for the conclusion of such agreements.

Convention No. 157 is considered to be an up to date instrument. However, it has been ratified by a rather peculiar group of not more than four States, members and non-members of the EU.[87]

ILO has in some cases convened a special conference to discuss a topic of interest to only a limited number of States. In the past those meetings concerned in particular European countries.[88] They resulted for example in the 1956 *European Convention concerning the social security of workers engaged in international transport*. It is opened for ratification by European ILO Member States and accession by all other European States.[89] It is restricted to co-ordination of legislation concerning short-term risks, i.e. sickness, maternity, industrial accidents, occupational diseases and death. It provides security without any condition as to nationality employees of any transport undertaking whose head office is located in the territory of a contracting party, working in the territory of one or more contracting States. It concerns land and water transport workers, with the exception of Rhine boatmen.

They are covered by a special *Agreement on Social Security for Rhine Boatmen* from 1950.[90] It has been adopted by a special tripartite conference convened in

86 Former Yugoslavia ratified the Convention No. 48 in 1945. Applicability for now independent States (Slovenia, Bosnia and Herzegovina, Croatia, Macedonia, Montenegro and Serbia) has been recognised in acts notifying its succession. *Bubnov Škoberne*, in Novak/Končar/Bubnov-Škoberne (eds.), 2006, p. 357, *Rismondo*, 2007, p. 654.

87 They are Spain, Sweden, Philippines and since 2008 Kyrgyzstan.

88 *Servais*, 2005, p. 63.

89 It has been ratified by current EU States (e.g. Belgium, France, Italy, Luxembourg, the Netherlands, Poland) and non-EU Member States (e.g. Turkey). *Valticos*, 1983, p. 139.

90 Concluded between EU Member States (e.g. Germany, Belgium, France, Luxembourg, the Netherlands) and non-EU States (Switzerland).

Geneva, by the Governing Body of the ILO. The initial agreement has been revised several times, also to take into account other co-ordination instruments like Regulation 1408/71 and the European Convention on Social Security. It is a complete agreement, covering all traditional social risks (also unemployment and family) and all co-ordination principles. The special Administrative Centre for social security of Rhine boatmen was established, which receives technical support from the ILO.[91]

Both instruments, covering workers in international transport and Rhine boatmen continue to apply also according to the Article 7 of the Regulation 1408/71.

3.3.2. Other ILO Conventions

Other ILO conventions, setting minimum standards, provide among others also for equality of treatment of nationals of contracting States. For example, Part XII of the *Social Security (Minimum Standards) Convention, 1952 (No. 102)*[92], requires equality of treatment of non-national residents. As a rule, they must have the same rights as national residents, especially in contributory schemes, i.e. in social insurance.

Similar provisions can be found in other ILO social security minimum standard conventions[93], but also conventions concerning migrant workers. For instance, according to the *Migration for Employment Convention (revised), 1949 (No. 97)*[94] social security law should apply to migrant workers without discrimination based on nationality. Appropriate arrangements may be undertaken for the maintenance of acquired rights and rights in course of acquisition, and special arrangements for non-contributory benefits.[95] Discrimination is also prohibited according to the *Migrant Workers (Supplementary Provisions) Convention, 1975 (No. 143).*[96]

3.4. MULTILATERAL INSTRUMENTS OF THE COUNCIL OF EUROPE

Not only the ILO, but also the Council of Europe (CoE) is one of the principal international organisations concerned with the production of multilateral social

---

91 Extensively on this agreement *Creutz*, 1981, p. 83 ff.

92 ILO Convention No. 102 has been ratified by 44 (EU and non-EU) States.

93 *Nussberger*, 2003, p. 1683.

94 Until the present 48 (EU and non-EU) States are bound by the Convention No. 97, among them e.g. Slovenia, Belgium, France, the Netherlands, Germany, Brazil, Cuba, Venezuela etc.

95 Article 6 (1 b) Convention No. 97.

96 Article 10 of the Convention No. 143, which is binding for 23 EU and non-EU States.

security co-ordination instruments that affect European (EU and non-EU) States. Yet, also other CoE instruments might be important for the co-ordination of social security systems, foremost among (some of) the 47 Member States.[97]

3.4.1. *Social Security Co-ordination Instruments*

Two European Interim Agreements[98] present the first step towards multilateral instruments of social security co-ordination by the CoE. Their structure and substance is very similar. However, there is an important difference in their material scope. The *European Interim Agreement on Social Security Schemes relating to Old-age, Invalidity and Survivors* covers long-term benefits, and the *European Interim Agreement on Social Security other then Schemes relating to Old-age, Invalidity and Survivors* covers short-term benefits. To each of the Interim Agreements a Protocol was added, extending their personal scope to refugees.

It was thought that some States might be prepared to accept co-ordination provisions in relation to short term benefits, but not to long term benefits. However in practice, all States that have ratified one of the Interim Agreements have also ratified the other.[99]

The European Interim Agreements are not all encompassing co-ordination instruments. They are restricted to the principle of equal treatment of nationals of other contracting parties with nationals of the State providing social security benefits. Nationals of all other contracting States have to be treated equally, as if they were own nationals of the State providing the benefits.[100] Moreover, advantages derived from bilateral or multilateral agreements on social security, concluded between two or more contracting parties are extended to nationals of all contracting States.[101]

The specific nature of the European Interim Agreements and their beauty is that they avoid the development of quite complex set of legal rules for establishing all basic principles of international social security co-ordination. Instead, they rely

---

97 The last to join was Montenegro in 2007. Some instruments are open to ratification to non-Members.

98 Signed in 1953 and in force since 1954. *Nickless/Siedl*, 2004, p. 22.

99 Lists of ratifications for both Interim Agreements, status as of 15 March 2009.

100 The principle of equal treatment is not absolute. The contracting States are free to exclude the principle of equal treatment in some areas or make it conditional in others. The conditions that may be imposed may vary according to the social risk covered and according to the legal nature of the scheme (i.e. being contributory or non-contributory one). *Strban*, 2006, pp. 11, 21.

101 Article 3 of both Interim Agreements.

upon existing social security mechanisms to ensure that an increased number of migrants receive proper protection.

Although, both European Interim Agreements are mainly dealing with only one co-ordination principle, they have an important legal impact due to the fact that many European (EU and non-EU) states have ratified them.[102]

As their name implies, the Interim Agreements were originally conceived as provisional measures. According to their preambles a general convention based on a network of bilateral agreements should be concluded. Accordingly, the European Convention on Social Security was designed to replace the interim agreements in relations between the contracting States. Yet, not all the contracting parties to the Interim Agreements have signed this Convention. Hence, Interim Agreements remain in force with a life of their own. A State may still choose to ratify one or both of the Interim Agreements, rather than the European Convention on Social Security.[103]

Additionally, accessions of the European States to the CoE, which are not yet members of the EU, have actually revived interest in the European Interim Agreements, which have been subject of an Explanatory Report.

The *European Convention on Social and Medical Assistance* was drawn up and signed at the same time as the European Interim Agreements. It is intended to operate alongside the two Interim Agreements, which exclude "public assistance". Hence, all three multilateral instruments complement each other in order to ensure the international co-ordination of the full range of social protection (social security and social assistance) schemes.[104] Like the two Interim Agreements, the European Convention on Social and Medical Assistance is also supplemented by a Protocol concerning the rights of refugees, and was subject to an Explanatory Report.

The basic principle of the Convention is the principle of equal treatment of nationals of all contracting States. They have to be entitled to the same social and medical assistance in the same amounts and under same conditions as own nationals of the State providing the assistance. To be granted equal access to social and medical assistance a person has to be not only a national of a contracting

---

102 In March 2009 Interim Agreements hold as much as 21 ratifications. Majority of them by EU Member States (Belgium, Cyprus, Czech Republic, Denmark, Estonia, France, Germany, Greece, Ireland, Italy, Latvia, Lithuania, Luxemburg, the Netherlands, Portugal, Spain, Sweden, United Kingdom), but also non-EU States (Iceland, Norway and Turkey).

103 Last ratification of Interim Agreements was in 2002 by Estonia.

104 In international law, clear distinction is made between social security (covering 9 traditional social security risks) and social assistance.

party, but also lawfully present in the territory of a State providing assistance and without sufficient resources.[105] The cost of assistance is born entirely by the State providing assistance. No requirement for the State of origin to refund the cost of assistance is stipulated.

One of the consequences of the non-discrimination principle is the prohibition of repatriation. State providing assistance is obliged not to repatriate from its territory a lawfully residing national of another contracting party just because he/she is in need of assistance.[106]

Like Interim Agreements, the European Convention on Social and Medical Assistance is mainly dealing with only one co-ordination principle. Its legal impact is not negligible, due to the fact that many European (EU and non-EU) states have ratified it.[107]

The *European Convention on Social Security* presents a much more comprehensive co-ordination mechanism, extending beyond the principle of equal treatment. It covers all traditional social security branches and co-ordination techniques.

Originally it was drafted during the 1960's by then 15 Member States to the CoE. It was opened for signature in 1972 and entered into force in 1977. By that time most of these States were also Members of the EU (then EEC), where social security co-ordination Regulations were in place. Hence, ratifying the Convention did not give much added value to the EU Member States. The resemblance between both co-ordination instruments is striking though, especially when one compares the original version of EC-Regulation 1408/71 with the European Convention on Social Security. The EC-regulation served to a great extent as a model for the co-ordination Convention of the CoE.[108]

Although, an all encompassing multilateral social security co-ordination instrument, the Convention has not been ratified by many EU and non-EU States[109], partially due to its special legal nature. It contains a mix of rules. Many

105 *Strban*, 2006, p. 34.
106 Article 6 of the European Convention on Social and Medical Assistance. However, prohibition of repatriation is not absolute.
107 In March 2009 the European Convention on Social and Medical Assistance holds 18 ratifications. Majority of them are by the EU Member States (Belgium, Denmark, Estonia, France, Germany, Greece, Ireland, Italy, Luxemburg, Malta, the Netherlands, Portugal, Spain, Sweden, United Kingdom), but also non-EU States (Iceland, Norway and Turkey). The last ratification was by Estonia in 2004.
108 *Schoukens*, 2006, p. 4.
109 The European Convention on Social Security has been ratified by only 8 States, members of the EU (Austria, Belgium, Italy, Luxembourg, the Netherlands, Portugal, Spain) and non-EU

of the provisions are directly applicable and hence can be directly invoked by the citizens as soon as the State ratifies the Convention. Articles that are not directly applicable represent suggestions or models for bilateral or multilateral agreements to be concluded between the contracting States implementing them. They leave the contracting States flexibility with regard to the eventual co-ordination techniques to be applied.[110]

The same goes for the Supplementary agreement for the application of the Convention, which covers its practical application. A Protocol was drafted in 1994, to extend the personal scope of the Convention, but it has not yet entered in force.[111]

3.4.2. *Other Social Security Instruments*

Although the European Code of Social Security (the Code), its Protocol and the European Code of Social Security (Revised) are not co-ordination, but rather harmonisation instruments, they touch also upon social security co-ordination.

The Code, for instance, encourages the contracting States to conclude a special instrument governing questions relating to social security for foreigners and migrants. With this instrument some of the basic principles of social security co-ordination should be applied, i.e. equality of treatment of nationals of other contracting States, protection of rights in course of acquisition and acquired rights.[112]

Although a more modern social security instrument, the revised Code has until now no ratifications (only 14 signatures by EU and non-EU States, e.g. Norway and Turkey). On the other hand, the initial Code has been widely ratified by EU and non-EU States directly.[113] Additionally, it represents a minimum standard of the revised European Social Charter.

States (Turkey). Additionally, it was signed by further 4 EU States (Czech Republic, France, Greece, Ireland) and 1 non-EU State (Moldova), not followed by ratification.

110 The application of special provisions concerning sickness and maternity, unemployment and family benefits, with the exception of the cumulation of periods, remains subject to the conclusion of bilateral or multilateral agreements between the States.

111 More also on the Explanatory Report and a Guide to the application of the Convention and the Supplementary Agreement *Nickless/Siedl*, 2004, p. 42 ff.

112 Article 73 of the Code.

113 The European Code of Social Security has been ratified by 20 EU and non-EU States (e.g. Slovenia, Belgium, Germany, France, the Netherlands, Norway, Switzerland, Turkey) and signed but not ratified by further 5 States (e.g. Moldova).

3.4.3. European Social Charter

The *European Social Charter* from 1961 and the *Revised European Social Charter* from 1996 are not specifically focused upon social security co-ordination. Moreover, they are not confined to social security at all. They contain goals and rights concerning (individual and collective) labour law and social protection (in the broad sense). Both Charters clearly distinguish between social security on one hand, and social and medical assistance on the other. The distinction is the same as in European Interim Agreements and European Convention on Social and Medical Assistance.

Article 12 of both Charters enshrines *the right to social security*. First three paragraphs are concerned with harmonisation of social security systems[114] and the fourth one with their co-ordination. The latter obliges the States, which have ratified it, to guarantee some of the basic principles of social security co-ordination, i.e. equal treatment, protection of acquired tights ("the retention of benefits") and protection of the rights in course of acquisition (by the "accumulation of insurance and employment periods").

European Social Charters do not establish a legally binding and directly applicable social security co-ordination mechanism. Contracting Sates have to "take steps" to ensure these principles. Hence they can be implemented by the conclusion of multilateral instruments and bilateral agreements or by other means. The supervisory body, i.e. the European Committee on Social Rights, has made it clear that other means may include unilateral measures[115] of the contracting State.

The Committee has closely scrutinised the endeavours of the States to fulfil their obligations under Article 12 of the Charters. It has established that the network of bilateral agreements, which vary greatly in their scope, is not complete. Also the existing ILO, CoE and EU multilateral instruments are insufficient, since they are not binding for all contracting States of the Charters.[116]

Article 13 of the European Social Charters enshrines *the right to social and medical assistance*. The contracting State should ensure it to any person without adequate resources or in need of necessary medical benefits. Especially the Paragraph 4 of this Article concerns co-ordination. The right should be provided on an equal footing to nationals of other contracting States lawfully within their territories, as

114 *Council of Europe*, 1999. p. 19.
115 *Ibidem*, p. 49.
116 *Ibidem*, p. 50 ff.

to their own nationals. Nationals of other contracting States should be treated in accordance with the provisions of the European Convention on Social and Medical Assistance. It is a standard of the Charters and it does not matter if the State is also bound by this Convention directly or not. This is why some States have not ratified Article 13 of the Charters in their full scope.[117]

The European Committee of Social Rights decided to make a clear distinction between those foreigners *lawfully residing* in the territory of another contracting State and those who are *lawfully present* there. The first are entitled to social and medical assistance in the same scope as resident nationals of a contracting State. Foreigners lawfully present are only entitled to emergency benefits that are designed to assist those in immediate need.[118]

It could be argued, that all nationals of other contracting States should be treated equally in social security and social assistance schemes, regardless if other States have ratified Articles 12 and 13 of the Charters or not. Coverage under these articles is *not subject to reciprocity*.[119] For instance, Croatia should provide social and medical assistance to Slovenian nationals, even if Slovenia has not ratified all paragraphs of Article 13.

Either one or both of the Charters have been ratified by all EU Member States and several non-EU States.[120]

3.4.4. European Convention of Human Rights

A counterpart to European Social Charters is the *European Convention of Human Rights* (ECHR). Although, it contains mainly civil and political rights, it is not unimportant for social security.[121] Concerning co-ordination of social security systems, the European Court of Human Rights (the Court) found provisions of national legislation refusing benefits to nationals of another CoE Member State on the sole ground of nationality contrary to the ECHR.

For instance, in the *Gaygusuz* case[122], the Turkish national applied for contributory benefit, i.e. emergency assistance after his entitlement to the unemployment

117 For instance, Slovenia has not ratified Paragraphs 1 and 4 of Article 13 Revised Charter.
118 *Nickless/Siedl*, 2004, p. 95.
119 *Council of Europe*, 1999, pp. 41 and 78.
120 For instance the initial European Social Charter was ratified by the non-EU States like Croatia (2003, without Article 12, but with Article 13) and Macedonia (2005, with both, Articles 12 and 13). The revised European Social Charter was ratified without Articles 12 and 13 by Albania (2002), Azerbaijan (2004), Ukraine (2006), Moldova (2001, without Article 13),with limitations to this Articles by Armenia (2004), Bosnia and Herzegovina (2008), and Georgia (2005).
121 Extensively in *Kapuy/Pieters/Zaglmayer*, 2007.
122 Gaygusuz v. Austria, 16 September 996, Appl. 17371/90.

benefit expired. It was refused based solely on lack of Austrian nationality. The Court found that difference in treatment between Austrians and non-Austrians is not based on any objective and reasonable justification. Hence, national legislation was in breach of Article 14 of the ECHR in conjunction with Article 1 of Protocol No.1.[123]

Similar decision was taken in the case *Koua Poirrez* in relation to non-contributory benefit.[124]

3.5. STABILISATION AND ASSOCIATION AGREEMENTS

It could be argued that *Stabilisation and Association Agreements* (SAA) concluded between the EC and its Member States on one hand and a non-EU State on the other are specific multilateral instruments. Among others, they contain certain norms relating to the co-ordination of social security systems.

They have been concluded with certain Maghreb States (e.g. Algeria, Morocco and Tunisia), Turkey[125] and in the years between 2001 and 2008 with some Western Balkan States (Macedonia, Croatia, Albania, Montenegro, Serbia, Bosnia and Herzegovina).

The provisions of the SAA's concluded with the Western Balkan States, dealing with social security co-ordination, are almost identical.[126] They provide for limited co-ordination (aggregation of periods and export of benefits), which is partially distinct from EC social security co-ordination Regulations.[127]

One of the basic questions is can a SAA be directly applicable. For instance, the ECJ has recognised direct applicability of Article 41 of the agreement with Morocco, as it contained a clear, precise and unconditional prohibition of

---

123 *Kapuy/Pieters/Zaglmayer*, 2007, p. 137.

124 *Kuoa Poirrez v. France*, 30 September 2003, Appl. 40892/98. In this case an allowance for the disabled adults was refused on the grounds that the applicant was neither a French national not a national of a country which had entered into a reciprocity agreement with France.

125 *Pennings*, 2003, p. 255.

126 The relations with Maghreb States and Turkey are subject of separate papers by colleagues *Verschueren* and *Aytek*.

127 For instance, periods within the EU should be aggregated, but not between the EU and non-EU contracting State, family members should be residing with the worker, unemployment benefits and sickness cash benefits are not mentioned (restriction of the material scope) and personal scope is limited to workers. Non-EU States should accord "similar" (not identical, but also not completely different) treatment to EU workers. E.g. Article 46 SAA (Macedonia), Article 47 SAA (Croatia), Article 51 SAA (Serbia), Article 48 SAA (Albania).

discrimination based on nationality in the social security field.[128] However, due to far reaching decisions of this judgment, the SAA's with Western Balkan States do not contain such or similar equal treatment provision.

The applicability of the SAA's is conditioned by the adoption of the Decision of the competent SAA Council. Hence, the next question is, can such decision be directly applicable in the EU Member States. For instance the Decision 3/80 of the Association Council EC-Turkey was not implemented by the contracting States. At first the ECJ established, that the Decision has no direct effect, since supplementary implementing measures have not been adapted by the Council.[129] Later on, it departed from this interpretation and recognised direct applicability to the principle of equal treatment in the field of social security.[130]

Proposed Decisions of SAA Councils with Western Balkan Countries, e.g. with Macedonia and Croatia[131], do not contain any equal treatment provisions being capable of having direct effect. Hence, it is obvious, when the ECJ gives a real meaning to a certain provision, the EU rather takes a step back.

These Decisions will still have to be implemented, probably with the EC regulation rather than legislative acts of the EU Member States. However, legislative action will probably be required on the side of the non-EU State. Due to the principle of reciprocity, probably not before the Decision of the SAA Council is implemented.[132]

4. CONCLUDING THOUGHTS

It could be argued, that bilateral social security agreements are not only the oldest, but remain the most important international instruments of social security co-ordination between EU and non-EU States, promoted also by some multilateral instruments. However, they do not create a common uniform co-ordination system, since bilateral agreements may be quite distinctive and limited to two contracting States. There is an obvious need for multilateral instruments.

---

128 *Kziber* (C-18/90), ECR 1991, p. I-199.

129 *Taflan-Met* (C-277/94), ECR, 1996, p. I-4085.

130 *Sürül* (C-262/96) ECR 1999, p. I-2685, *Kocak and Örs* (C-102/98 and C-211/98) ECR 2000, p. I-1287, *Oztürk* (C-373/02), ECR 2004, p. I-3605.

131 COM(2007) 787 final, COM(2007) 789 final.

132 *Strban*, March 2006, p. 26.

Social security co-ordination norms can be found in many distinctive multilateral instruments dealing specifically with social security (co-ordination) or not. However, multilateral instruments are either outdated, incomplete, i.e. dealing only with one social security co-ordination principle, or ratified by very few non-EU States. Even if Courts of Law (on national or European Community level) actually give some meaning to multilateral instruments, they are either denounced or such provisions are omitted in the new agreements.

Hence, despite a large number of various international social security co-ordination instruments, influenced also by the EC social security law, the situation is hardly satisfactory. It could be argued, that the existing bilateral and multilateral instruments binding EU and non-EU States do not ensure proper enjoyment of the universal right to social security. Universal social security co-ordination scheme might be required.

BIBLIOGRAPHY

BMAS – Bundesministerium für Arbeit und Soziales, Zweiseitige Abkommen, www.bmas.de.

Creutz, Helmut: The new Agreement on Social Security for Rhine Boatmen, International Labour Review, No. 1/1981, p. 83–96.

Council of Europe: Social protection in the European Social Charter, Council of Europe Publishing, Strasbourg, 1999.

Eichenhofer, Eberhard: Internationales Sozialrecht, C.H. Beck, München, 1994.

Kapuy, Klaus, Pieters, Danny, Zaglmayer, Bernhard: Social Security Cases in Europe: The European Court of Human Rights, Intersentia, Antwerpen-Oxford, 2007.

Ministry of Overseas Indian Affairs, www.moia.gov.in.

Nickless, Jason, Siedl, Helmut: Co-ordination of Social Security in the Council of Europe: Short Guide, Council of Europe Publishing, Strasbourg, 2004.

Novak, Mitja, Končar, Polonca, Bubnov Škoberne, Anjuta (eds.) et.al., Konvencije Mednarodne organizacije dela s komentarjem, GV Založba, Ljubljana, 2006.

Nussberger, Angelika: Das Sozialrecht der internationalen Organisationen, in Bernd Baron von Maydell/Franz Ruland (HRSG.), Sozialrechtshandbuch (SRH), Nomos, Baden-Baden, 2003, p. 1677–1700.

Pennings, Frans: An Overview of Interpretation issues of International Social Security Standards, in Pennings, F. (ed.), International Social Security Standards, Intersentia, Antwerp-Oxford, 2007, p. 1–31.

Pennings, Frans: The Impact of Social Securitiy Conventions: The Netherlands, in Pennings, F. (ed.), Between Soft and Hard Law, Kluwer Law International, 2006, p. 85–113.

Pennings, Frans: Introduction to European Social Security Law, Intersentia, Antwerp-Oxford-New York, 2003.

Pennings, Frans, Shulte, Bernd: International Social Security Standards: An Overview, in Pennings, F. (ed.), Between Soft and Hard Law, Kluwer Law International, 2006, p. 1–26.

Perrin, Guy: Die Ursprünge des internationalen Rechts der sozialen Sicherheit, VSSR Beiheft 3, J. Schweitzer Verlag, München, 1983.

Petersen, Ulrich: Sozialversicherungsabkommen, in Bernd Baron von Maydell/ Franz Ruland (HRSG.), Sozialrechtshandbuch (SRH), Nomos, Baden-Baden, 2003, pp. 1701–1723.

Pieters, Danny: Social Security: An Introduction to the Basic Principles, Kluwer Law International, 2006.

Rismondo, Mihovil: Zbirka ugovora o socialnom osiguranju, Narodne novine, Zagreb, 2007.

Roberts, Simon: Migration and social security: Parochialism in the global village, ISSA, The Year 2000 International Research Conference on Social Security, Helsinki, 2000.

Servais, Jean-Michel: International Labour law, Kluwer Law International, 2005.

Schoukens, Paul: Acceding to the multilateral co-ordination Convention on Social Security: Consequences for the social security legislation of the involved SISP-parties (Albania, Croatia, BIH, Kosovo, Serbia and Montenegro), Leuven, 2006, www.coe.int.

Schoukens, Paul: Introduction to Social security Co-ordination in the EU, in Pieters, D., Shoukens, P. (eds.), European Social Security Law, Institute of Social Law, Leuven, 2004–2005, p. 103–165.

Schulte, Bernd: Treatment of Third-country Nationals in the Member States of the EU and the EEA in terms of Social Law (Same treatment as Nationals?), German National Report, in B. von Maydell/B. Schulte (eds.), Treatment of Third-country Nationals in the EU and EEA Member States in terms of Social Security Law, Peeters, Leuven, 1995, p. 105–139.

Steinmeyer, Heinz-Dietrich: Das nationale Recht grenzüberschreitender Sachverhalte, in Bernd Baron von Maydell/Franz Ruland (HRSG.), Sozialrechtshandbuch (SRH), Nomos, Baden-Baden, 2003, p. 1583–1609.

Strban, Grega: Examination of the CARDS-SISP Countries' Social Security Systems in comparison with the Council of Europe's Interim Agreements and the European Convention on Social and Medical Assistance, Ljubljana, 2006, www.coe.int.

Strban, Grega: Examination of The Macedonian Legislation in the Social Security Field in comparison with the EC Regulations on Co-ordination of Social Security Schemes, Ljubljana, March 2006.

Türk, Danilo: Temelji mednarodnega prava, GV Založba, Ljubljana, 2007.

Valticos, Nicolas: Droit International du Travail, Dalloz, Paris, 1983.

Vonk, Gijsbert, Migration, Social Security and the Law, in J. Berghman et.al. (eds.), Social Security in Transition, Kluwer Law International, The Hague, 2002, p. 77–91.

Vonk, Gijsbert, Report on the relevance of the EU legislation for the social security rights of persons from SISP countries who move between the Balkan region and the EU Member States, Amstelveen, 2006, www.coe.int.

EUROPEAN AND INTERNATIONAL LAW IN RELATION TO THE SOCIAL SECURITY OF IRREGULAR MIGRANT WORKERS

KLAUS KAPUY*

1. INTRODUCTION

This contribution investigates to what extent European and international legislation makes a statement on the social security of irregular migrant workers. In doing so, the focus will be on social security rights, i.e. on the protection granted to these workers.

In this introduction, I will outline what I understand by the terms 'irregular migrant worker' and 'social security, why it is of interest to examine the European and international legal framework and what the scope of this investigation will be.

Most people have already heard about illegal, irregular, unauthorized or undocumented migrants. When these terms are used, it is usually referred to non-nationals who enter, stay and/or work in a country in violation of national or international legislation. This contribution will in particular focus on non-citizens who are economically active in the host country; to be more precise, on non-citizens who are being employed in the host country, without being allowed to do so, simply because they are no citizens. So it will be about employed and not about self-employed individuals. Often, such non-citizens also do not have a permission to stay in the country of work. However, this is not necessarily the case. This article will therefore cover two different groups. First, those who work unlawfully and stay unlawfully in a country. These are, for instance, aliens who clandestinely enter the country and take up employment in violation of the laws. But they can

* Klaus Kapuy is a PhD candidate at the Institute of Social Law of the Catholic University of Leuven. The author welcomes feedback and may be contacted at the following address: Blijde Inkomststraat 17, 3000 Leuven, Belgium; e-mail: klaus.kapuy@law.kuleuven.be. The author acknowledges with thanks the advice of Paul Schoukens. All statements in this work are as at 1 May 2009.

also be tourists who overstay their visas and subsequently stay and work unlawfully. And, second, those who work unlawfully, but stay lawfully in the host country. Examples are students or family members who have the right to reside (and study) in the host country, but not the right to take up employment.

Another crucial concept used in this contribution is the one of social security. Under social security I understand a statutory system based on the principle of solidarity, which provides protection against (the threat of) a lack of income or against particular costs in case of the occurrence of a recognised social risk.[1] Both main social security techniques, i.e. social insurance and social assistance, are taken on board.

Why is it of interest to investigate the European and international legal framework? We have seen that national governments struggle with the question of the right dose of social protection to be granted to individuals staying on their soil illegally and/or working there illegally. Arguments put forward to extend the social protection of this group of people mostly relate to the idea of human rights. It is argued that irregular migrant workers are human beings and therefore they should be protected by human rights, as laid down in international, European and national legislation. By contrast, advocates of a restriction of protection usually make the point that this group is not allowed to stay and/or work in the country. As a consequence, no or only limited rights must arise, otherwise there would be no coherence in state action. In the vast majority of countries, there is a further dimension added to this discussion. Irregular work by foreigners is usually associated with undeclared work; meaning that social security contributions are not paid and the proper functioning of the social security system is threatened. It is therefore interesting to know what guidance European and international law gives on this issue. Or, in other words, which limits are set for the national legislator.

As for the scope of the analysis, at the universal level multilateral instruments of the United Nations, as well as the International Labour Organization (as a specialized agency of the United Nations) are taken on board. At the European level, supranational law of the European Union and law of the Council of Europe will be discussed. It is important to note that I distinguish, on the one hand, between the universal level and the European level, which relates to the geographical impact of multilateral legal instruments; and on the other hand, between international law, i.e. law of international organisations, and supranational law, i.e. European Community Law.

---

1 For this definition see Danny Pieters, *Social Security: An introduction to the basic principles*. 2. ed. (Alphen aan den Rijn: Kluwer Law International, 2006), 2, 3.

The analysis will start with human rights law; beginning with general and specific human rights treaties at the universal level and addressing then human rights law in Europe. Thereafter, we will turn to universal and European treaties which particularly deal with the legal status of migrant workers. This is followed by an investigation on social security standard setting treaties. And finally, European Union law which may be relevant for the social security of irregular migrant workers will be addressed.

When analysing these legal instruments, their interpretation by international courts and supervisory bodies will be taken into consideration. Excluded, however, will be their interpretation by national courts or national authorities.

Due to space constraints, a selection had to be made with regard to the international and European Community legislation included in this analysis. What will not be part of this investigation is social security co-ordination law. Moreover, special international and European Community legislation dealing with refugees, asylum seekers and stateless persons will also not be included.

2. HUMAN RIGHTS LAW

The idea behind analysing the universal and European human rights framework is the assumption that irregular migrant workers are human beings and might thus also have human rights. Most notably, the question is whether this group enjoys human rights which are related to their social security.

2.1. UNIVERSAL LEVEL

2.1.1. General Human Rights Treaties

The first set of treaties to be analysed is the International Bill of Human Rights. It consists of the Universal Declaration of Human Rights 1948[2], the International Covenant on Economic, Social and Cultural Rights 1966[3] and the International Covenant on Civil and Political Rights 1966.[4]

---

2 Universal Declaration of Human Rights, UN General Assembly resolution 217A (III), 10 December 1948.

3 International Covenant on Economic, Social and Cultural Rights, UN General Assembly resolution 2200A (XXI), 16 December 1966, entry into force 3 January 1976.

4 International Covenant on Civil and Political Rights, UN General Assembly resolution 2200A (XXI), 16 December 1966, entry into force 23 March 1976.

The Universal Declaration of Human Rights (UDHR) stipulates in Article 22 that "*[e]veryone*, as a member of society, has the right to social security [emphasis added by the author]". Moreover, Article 25 reads that "*[e]veryone* has the right to a standard of living adequate for the health and well-being of himself and of his family [emphasis added by the author]".[5]

Similarly, Article 9 of the International Covenant on Economic, Social and Cultural Rights (ICESCR) obliges states parties to recognise the right of *everyone* to social security, including social insurance. In addition, Articles 11 and 12 lay down the right of *everyone* to an adequate standard of living for himself and his family and the right of *everyone* to the enjoyment of the highest attainable standard of physical and mental health.

Both documents, the UDHR and the ICESCR grant these rights to everyone and make no further distinction as to nationality. Let alone a distinction based on the immigration status of an alien. And also the phrase 'member of society' does not shed any light on the situation of irregular migrant workers. However, in 1985, some decades after the adoption of these human rights documents, the General Assembly of the UN adopted the Declaration on the Human Rights of Individuals Who are not Nationals of the Country in which They Live.[6] This declaration further specifies, restricts and extends human rights to aliens. Whereas the declaration confirms the unrestricted application of certain civil rights, such as the right to life, the right to family and private life or the prohibition of torture to all aliens, it confines the application of, in particular, social rights only to aliens lawfully residing in the territory of a state. This is, most notably, the case for the UDHR's and ICESCR's rights to social security, social services, medical care and health protection.[7] Not only that these rights are being made subject to a lawful stay, they are also being made subject to a general compliance with the laws of the state in which they reside or are present.[8] This would indicate that states do not have to grant these social rights in case of violation of alien employment laws.

It is interesting to note that one of the main reasons for elaborating this declaration was exactly to address the uncertainty surrounding the application of the International Bill of Human Rights to aliens. Whereas some commentators

5 This includes, amongst others, medical care, necessary social services and the right to security in the event of unemployment, sickness, disability, old age and so on.

6 See Declaration on the Human Rights of Individuals Who are not Nationals of the Country in which They Live, Annex to the UN General Assembly resolution 40/144, 13 December 1985. It has to be noted that this is no legally binding document.

7 § 8 (1)(c) Declaration on the Human Rights of Individuals Who are not Nationals of the Country in which They Live.

8 § 8 (1) in conjunction with § 4 Declaration on the Human Rights of Individuals Who are not Nationals of the Country in which They Live.

argued that the wording *everyone* leaves no doubt that non-citizens are also addressed, others saw in the lack of the ground *nationality* as a prohibited ground for discrimination in the relevant international treaties evidence that non-citizens are not included (more on discrimination later on).[9] The declaration was intended to clarify this ambiguity. And by doing so, it further distinguished between lawfully and unlawfully staying aliens.

So, according to the General Assembly Declaration of 1985 unlawfully staying foreigners are *explicitly* excluded and unlawfully working foreigners are *implicitly* excluded from the enjoyment of all social security related human rights.

A more differentiated approach can be observed in the past decade. The Committee on Economic, Social and Cultural Rights, which monitors the implementation of the ICESCR, regularly provides guidelines for states parties on the interpretation of the ICESCR. Regarding social security related rights, five so-called General Comments have been issued. The first three were produced in the 1990s and concerned the right to adequate housing and the right to adequate food.[10] There, the issue of irregularly residing and/or working foreigners was not addressed.[11] The later two General Comments, by contrast, did so. General Comment No. 14 on the right to health, which was published in 2000, obliges state parties to refrain from denying or limiting equal access of all persons to preventive, curative and palliative health services. It is expressly mentioned that the phrase 'all persons' includes illegal immigrants.[12] As an example of a violation of this obligation the General Comment names the "denial of access to health facilities, goods and services to particular individuals or groups as a result of de jure or de facto discrimination". Last year, General Comment No. 19 on the right to social security was published.[13] Also here illegal migrants were expressly taken into consideration

---

9 For more information on this historical debate see Carmen Tiburcio, *The human rights of aliens under international and comparative law* (The Hague/Boston/London: Martinus Nijhoff Publishers, 2001), 56.

10 Committee on Economic, Social and Cultural Rights, *General Comment No. 4: The right to adequate housing (Art.11 (1))*, E/1992/23 (New York: United Nations, 1991); Committee on Economic, Social and Cultural Rights, *General Comment No. 7: The right to adequate housing (Art.11 (1)): forced evictions*, E/1998/22 (New York: United Nations, 1997); and Committee on Economic, Social and Cultural Rights, *General Comment No. 12: The right to adequate food (Art.11)*, E/C.12/1999/5 (New York: United Nations, 1999).

11 General Comment No. 4 refers in § 6 to "individuals, as well as families, are entitled to adequate housing regardless of age, economic status, group or other affiliation or status and other such factors". Although not expressly mentioned, this could possibly also refer to migrants with an irregular immigration status.

12 Committee on Economic, Social and Cultural Rights, *General Comment No. 14: The right to the highest attainable standard of health (Art.12)*, E/C.12/2000/4 (New York: United Nations, 2000), § 34.

13 Committee on Economic, Social and Cultural Rights, *General Comment No. 19: The right to social security (Art.9)*, E/C.12/GC/19 (New York: United Nations, 2008).

when it comes to health care. Section 37 stipulates that "[a]ll persons, irrespective of their nationality, residency or immigration status, are entitled to primary and emergency medical care."

It must be appreciated that the Committee on Economic, Social and Cultural Rights also addressed the issue of irregular migrants. Unfortunately, in doing so it worked with a diffuse terminology. So that at the end of the day it is not clear what the right to health for individuals with an irregular immigration status really comprises.

Let me give some examples. What does 'refrain from denying or limiting equal access to health services' or 'entitlement to medical care' exactly mean? Is it about getting treated or also about getting the costs of treatment covered? It seems that, at least, General Comment No. 19 includes cost coverage. In the introduction to General Comment No. 19 the following is stipulated:

> "[t]he right to social security encompasses the right to access and maintain benefits, whether in cash or in kind, without discrimination in order to secure protection, inter alia, from (a) lack of work-related income caused by sickness, disability, maternity, employment injury, unemployment, old age, or death of a family member; (b) unaffordable access to health care; (c) insufficient family support, particularly for children and adult dependents."[14]

So it is about the protection against unaffordable access to health care and not just against non-access to health care. This could be evidence that 'entitlement to primary and emergency medical care' under section 37 of General Comment No. 19 should be interpreted as also covering the costs of the treatment.

It is also not clear what is to be understood by the term 'primary care'. This is not defined in the General Comment. Is it the first point of consultation for patients? Or is it all non-hospital care? In addition, one can ask whether primary care, whatever it means, must include an element of necessity or urgency. Or does the Committee on Economic, Social and Cultural Rights consider all forms of primary care, even if medically not necessary, as being granted under the ICESCR?

Moreover, there is another big weakness of these General Comments. The Committee consisting of experts does not explain how it reaches its conclusions: how come the Committee finds a right to this and that degree of health care for individuals irrespective their immigration status? There is no explanation at all. And then one can find him- or herself in the situation where he or she can ask: has this really been provided for in the legal text? *Paul Schoukens* has warned on many

---

14 *Ibid.*, § 2.

occasions that, in general, a lack of explanation combined with an extensive interpretation carries the danger that the legal value of the Convention will be undermined. Contracting states may challenge the interpretative authority of the Committee and may not follow its interpretation anymore.[15] In particular in the context of non-citizens with an irregular status of stay or work in a country, contracting states may be interested to know how the Committee reached its conclusions. This is so because the UN General Assembly, and therefore also the contracting states, explicitly excluded in 1985 non-citizens with an unlawful stay from the right to medical care. But this 1985 declaration is not at all mentioned in the Committee's General Comment No. 19. This could be regarded as an obvious neglect of the will of the contracting states and indeed carries the danger that states are not following this interpretation.

If we analyse the rest of General Comment No. 19 on the right to social security, we can see that there is no further reference made to individuals with an irregular immigration status. Sometimes there is a reference made to non-nationals. But then it is not clear whether non-nationals with an irregular residence status or migrant workers who work in violation of immigration laws are included.

As I already indicated before, all three UN human rights treaties include non-discrimination provisions. Non-discrimination might be of interest for irregular migrants and their access to social security. Depending on the concrete circumstances, their situation could be compared to the one of citizens, of regular migrants or – and this might be of particular relevance when it comes to social security related to work – of black economy workers.[16]

But we always have to be aware that the principle of equal treatment or non-discrimination requires a comparable situation. This means two individuals must be in a situation of similar circumstances. Thereafter, one can look if they, despite theses similar circumstances, are treated differently. And finally it is to evaluate if this difference in treatment can be, mostly objectively and reasonably, justified. Regarding irregular migrant workers, I do not see them per se in a comparable situation with citizens or migrants with a regular status of stay and work. This would depend on the individual circumstances. For instance, one can argue that an irregular migrant worker who:

---

15 See, inter alia, Paul Schoukens, "Recht op gezondheidszorg volgens het internationale socialezekerheidsrecht," *Tijdschrift voor gezondheidsrecht* 2 (2008/2009): 107.

16 Paul Schoukens and Danny Pieters advocate for a comparison with nationals who work in the black economy. See Paul Schoukens and Danny Pieters, *Exploratory Report on the Access to Social Protection for Illegal Labour Migrants* (Strasbourg: Council of Europe, 2004), 6, 27, 34, 35.

- has resided for a long period of time in the country of work;
- has built up an economic and a social link with the country of work; and
- has not paid any social insurance contributions during his or her employment.

could be compared to a citizen of that country who works in the black economy, i.e. who does not pay any social insurance contributions. This says nothing about justification. Maybe there are reasons to justify a different treatment of these two groups. Still, under above mentioned circumstances, there are at least good reasons to assume that an irregular migrant worker is in an analogous situation to a citizen who works in the black economy.

The question is now whether the non-discrimination provisions of the International Bill of Human Rights would provide a basis for an equal treatment examination. What is striking is that all three documents do not explicitly regard citizenship or nationality as a prohibited ground of discrimination.[17] The ground 'national origin' is sometimes interpreted to be equivalent to citizenship. But in fact, it is more likely that it refers to national characteristics.[18] However, because the list of prohibited grounds is not exhaustive in any of the Bill's non-discrimination provisions[19], one can argue that citizenship, residence status or work status could be regarded as further grounds. And indeed, Article 26 of the International Covenant on Civil and Political Rights (ICCPR), which can be considered as an autonomous non-discrimination provision – i.e. it applies to all discrimination by a state, even beyond the civil and political rights enumerated in the ICCPR – has been interpreted by the Human Rights Committee to also protect against discrimination based on citizenship.[20] The same can probably be said about the non-discrimination provision of the ICESR, although there is no absolute certainty yet.[21] From this it follows that the UN Bill of Human Rights could be

17 See § 2 (2) ICESCR, § 2 (1) ICCPR, § 26 ICCPR, § 2 UDHR.

18 UN Commission on Human Rights, Sub-Commission on Prevention of Discrimination and Protection of Minorities, *International provisions protecting the human rights of non-citizens*, study prepared by Baroness Elles, Special Rapporteur, UN Doc. E/CN.4/Sub.2/392/Rev.I (1980) I (New York: United Nations, 1980), § 114.

19 There is however some discussion as to § 2 (2) ICESCR. Here some commentators argue that this list is indeed exhaustive and leaves no room for further prohibited grounds. For a discussion see Ryszard Cholewinski, *Migrant workers in international human rights law: Their protection in countries of employment* (Oxford: Clarendon Press, 1997), 57, 58.

20 See Human Rights Committee, *General Comment No. 15: The position of aliens under the Covenant*, in compilation of General Comments and General Recommendations adopted by Human Rights Treaty Bodies, UN Doc HRI/GEN/1/Rev.8 (New York: United Nations, 2006). See also Human Rights Committee in Josef Frank Adam v. The Czech Republic, Communication No. 586/1994, U.N. Doc. CCPR/C/57/D/586/1994 (1996).

21 For a discussion see Ryszard Cholewinski, *Migrant workers in international human rights law: Their protection in countries of employment* (Oxford: Clarendon Press, 1997), 58. The Committee on Economic, Social and Cultural Rights stipulates in general comment No. 19

invoked for an equal treatment assessment concerning irregular migrant workers and their social security.

2.1.2. *Specific Human Rights Treaties*

Beside general human rights treaties, the UN has adopted treaties dealing with the human rights of particular groups. Leaving aside for now the UN Migrant Worker Convention, I will discuss below the International Convention on the Elimination of All Forms of Racial Discrimination 1965, the Convention on the Elimination of All Forms of Discrimination against Women 1979 and the Convention on the Rights of the Child 1989. These special human rights instruments provide for non-discrimination and also for a right to social security. Similar to the International Bill of Human Rights, in the documents themselves there is no reference made to irregular migrant workers. What we however can see is that the guidelines for the interpretation of these documents – this means the General Comments and General Recommendations –, directly address the issue of irregular migrant workers.

The oldest of these conventions, the International Convention on the Elimination of All Forms of Racial Discrimination (CERD), requires contracting states to prohibit and eliminate racial discrimination in all its forms and to guarantee "the right of everyone, without distinction as to race, colour, or national or ethnic origin, to equality before the law, notably in the enjoyment of [...] [t]he right to housing; [t]he right to public health, medical care, social security and social services".[22] Pursuant to Article 1(2) CERD, the Convention "shall not apply to distinctions, exclusions, restrictions or preferences made [...] between citizens and non-citizens". This, however, does not mean that the CERD is not applicable to non-citizens. It only means that a distinction purely based on nationality does not come within the ambit of this Convention. There must also be an element of racial discrimination.[23]

that "Article 2, paragraph 2, prohibits discrimination on grounds of nationality". This, however, comes out of the blue. Does the committee consider 'national origin' as nationality or does it regard 'other status' as nationality? See Committee on Economic, Social and Cultural Rights, *General Comment No. 19: The right to social security (Art.9)*, E/C.12/GC/19 (New York: United Nations, 2008), § 36.

22 See § 5 (e) (iii) and (iv) International Convention on the Elimination of All Forms of Racial Discrimination, UN General Assembly resolution 2106 (XX), 21 December 1965.

23 The Committee on the Elimination of Racial Discrimination stipulates in General Recommendation No. 30 that "under the Convention, differential treatment based on citizenship or immigration status will constitute discrimination if the criteria for such differentiation, judged in the light of the objectives and purposes of the Convention, are not applied pursuant to a legitimate aim, and are not proportional to the achievement of this aim". See Committee on the Elimination of Racial Discrimination, *General Recommendation No. 30: Discrimination against no non citizens* (New York: United Nations, 2005), § 4.

In General Recommendation No. 30, the Committee on the Elimination of Racial Discrimination advanced the opinion that the Convention is also applicable to migrants with an irregular migration status. In more detail, in section 7 the Committee recommends that state parties shall "[e]nsure that legislative guarantees against racial discrimination apply to non-citizens regardless of their immigration status, and that the implementation of legislation does not have a discriminatory effect on non-citizens". Therefore, according to the wording of the Convention and the interpretation of the Committee, racial discrimination in the field of social security – both in the implementation of social security legislation or in the law itself – is not allowed and must be prevented; and this regardless of the immigration status of a person.

The Convention on the Elimination of All Forms of Discrimination against Women (CEDAW) obliges state parties to eliminate discrimination against women in the field of social security.[24] In December 2008, the Committee on the Elimination of Discrimination against Women issued General Recommendation No. 26 on women migrant workers.[25] The Committee made clear that the Convention applies to migrant women in general. But due to the fact that migrant women who are taking up employment in the country of destination are at a higher risk of abuse and discrimination, particular attention has been paid to women migrant workers.[26] The Recommendation distinguishes between women migrant workers and undocumented women migrant workers. The latter group is defined as migrant workers who are without a valid residence or work permit.[27] Subsection 26(1) of the General Recommendation lays down that "[r]egardless of the lack of immigration status of undocumented women migrant workers, States parties have an obligation to protect their basic human rights". What these basic human rights are as regards social security is somewhat intricately formulated: it is stipulated that "[u]ndocumented women migrant workers must have access to legal remedies and justice [...] if they [...] face deprivation of fulfilment of basic needs, including in times of health emergencies or pregnancy or maternity, or if they are abused physically or sexually by employers or others".[28] This is about access to justice to enforce the rights. This presupposes, of course, that they have the rights to fulfilment of needs in case of health emergencies, pregnancy, maternity or abuse. But this seems to be taken for granted here. In another section

24 § 11 (1) (e); § 11 (2) (b) and (c); § 12 (1); § 13 (a); § 14 (2) (b), (c) and (h) Convention on the Elimination of All Forms of Discrimination against Women, UN General Assembly resolution, 34/180, 18 December 1979.

25 Committee on the Elimination of Discrimination against Women, *General Recommendation No. 26 on women migrant workers*, CEDAW/C/2009/WP.1/R (New York: United Nations, 2008).

26 *Ibid.*, § 4.

27 *Ibid.*

28 *Ibid.*, § 26 (1).

of the Recommendation, we can find the responsibility of the country of destination to provide victims of abuse with relevant emergency and social services, regardless of their immigration status.[29] Unfortunately, there is no further specification as to what emergency and social services are. In its Recommendation, the Committee gives a kind of general explanation of the specific circumstances and the particular vulnerability of documented and undocumented women migrant workers. This explains why the Committee decided to interpret the Convention as also applying to female migrant workers with an irregular status of residence or work. It would nevertheless have been interesting to know how it reached its conclusion to explicitly grant legal remedies in times of health emergencies, pregnancy, maternity or abuse and emergency and social services for victims of abuse.

The third convention, i.e. the Child Rights Convention (CRC), includes a number of rights related to social security.[30] Most notably the right to health[31], the right to social security (including social insurance)[32] and the right to an adequate standard of living.[33] Moreover, Article 2 forbids discrimination with respect to the rights set forth in the Convention. Once more nationality is not explicitly listed as a prohibited ground. But also once more, the list of prohibited grounds is illustrative only.

In 2005, the Committee on the Rights of the Child issued General Comment No. 6 on the treatment of unaccompanied and separated children outside their country of origin.[34] The Committee lay down that the enjoyment of the rights stipulated in the Convention must be available to all children, including migrant children – irrespective of their nationality, immigration status or statelessness.[35] The Committee deduced this point of view from the wording of Article 2(1) CRC – the Convention's non-discrimination provision. There it is written that the contracting states must respect and ensure the rights set forth in the Convention without discrimination to "each child within their jurisdiction".

Looking back on the social protection of irregular migrant workers under the United Nations universal human rights instruments, I conclude that most of the

29 *Ibid.*, § 26 (i).
30 Convention on the Rights of the Child, UN General Assembly resolution 44/25, 20 November 1989.
31 § 24 CRC.
32 § 26 CRC.
33 § 27 CRC.
34 Committee on the Rights of the Child, *General Recommendation No. 6: Treatment of unaccompanied and separated children outside their country of origin*, CRC/GC/2005/6 (New York: United Nations, 2005).
35 *Ibid.*, § 12.

instruments themselves talk about protection for everyone. Differentiation regarding citizenship or immigration status is not made. Only the 1985 Declaration on the Human Rights of Individuals Who are not Nationals of the Country in which They Live makes a clear distinction between lawfully and unlawfully residing aliens. Under this declaration, unlawfully residing aliens are completely excluded from the right to medical care, social security and social services. If we however look at the interpretation of the legally binding human rights conventions – i.e. the ICESCR, CERD, CEDAW and CRC – by the competent committees, we can see that a more elaborated approach has been taken. Yet this is only true for the past decade. Before the year 2000, no reference was made to the rights of irregular migrant workers. From 2000 on, the human rights treaties have been interpreted as also containing rights concerning the social security of non-citizens with an irregular status of stay or work. This has most notably been the case with the right to health.

2.2. EUROPEAN LEVEL

On the European level I want to focus on two human rights treaties: the European Social Charter (ESC) and the European Convention on Human Rights (ECHR). Both were adopted under the authority of the Council of Europe.

The European Social Charter guarantees economic and social human rights.[36] It was adopted in 1961 and was revised in 1996. The original and the revised document are two distinctive treaties, but still resemble each other in the field of social security. There are four provisions I want to emphasise: Articles 12 and 13 of both ESCs as well as Article 17 and Article E of the RESC. Article 12 stipulates, most notably, that the parties undertake "to establish or maintain a system of social security". Article 13 establishes the right to social and medical assistance and requires the parties to undertake "to ensure that any person who is without adequate resources [...] be granted adequate assistance, and, in case of sickness, the care necessitated by his condition". And Article 17 of the RESC obliges state parties to take measures "to ensure that children and young persons [...] have the care, the assistance [...] they need". Moreover, Article E of the RESC provides for the principle of non-discrimination as regards the rights set forth in the Charter. The prohibited grounds do not explicitly include nationality or immigration status. However, since it is an open list, nothing would preclude an interpretation in this direction.

36 European Social Charter, 18 October 1961, ETS No.035 and European Social Charter (revised), 3 May 1996, ETS No. 163.

Out of these four provisions, only in Article 13 – the right to social and medical assistance – is there a special reference made to lawfully staying aliens. Paragraph 4 rules that contracting states must apply this article "on an equal footing with their nationals to nationals of other Parties lawfully within their territories".

But this is not the only reference made to a lawful immigration status. The beginning of the Appendices to both versions of the ESC reads as follows:

> "Without prejudice to Article 12, paragraph 4, and Article 13, paragraph 4, the persons covered by Articles 1 to 17 [and 20 to 31] include foreigners only in so far as they are nationals of other [Contracting] Parties lawfully resident or working regularly within the territory of the Party concerned, subject to the understanding that these articles are to be interpreted in the light of the provisions of Articles 18 and 19."

Article 18 intends to facilitate the free movement of workers between state parties. And Article 19 grants certain protection and assistance to migrant workers, such as for instance the protection against misleading propaganda relating to emigration and immigration.

So, on the whole, irregular migrant workers do not enjoy the social rights enshrined in the (R)ESC. But, as stipulated in the Appendices, the exclusion is without prejudice to Articles 12(4) and 13(4). What is stipulated in these two articles?

Article 12(4) (R)ESC requires the state parties to elaborate through bilateral and multilateral agreements social security co-ordination rules for migrant workers. But the exact conditions of this co-ordination are left to the discretion of the state parties. So, contracting states have the possibility to derive from the requirement of lawful residence or lawful work, as laid down in the Appendices, when working out co-ordination instruments.

Article 13(4) (R)ESC, as illustrated before, rules that the right to social and medical assistance must be equally applied to the own citizens and to citizens of other state parties, provided that they are lawfully within the territory. So, while it is in general required that a national of another contracting state lawfully *resides* or works in order to enjoy the social rights set forth in the charter, for social and medical assistance only lawful *presence* is demanded. According to the European Committee of Social Rights, which supervises the implementation of the (R)ESC, this should be interpreted as a coverage of two different categories of foreigners under Article 13: first, those who are, according to the Appendices, lawfully residing or lawfully working and, second, those who are, pursuant to Article 13(4)

(R)ESC, lawfully present without lawfully residing or lawfully working.[37] As regards the latter, the Committee emphasises that it is about individuals whose stay is only temporary, such as tourists or students. Accordingly, for this group "the most appropriate form of assistance would be emergency aid to enable them to cope with an immediate state of need (accommodation, food, emergency care and clothing)".[38]

Therefore, according to the wording of the European Social Charter and the Revised European Social Charter, irregular migrant workers are excluded from above mentioned social rights. But this is not exactly how the European Committee of Social Rights has interpreted the Charter regarding unlawfully residing non-citizens.

In a collective complaint by an international non-governmental organisation against France, the Committee was in 2004 confronted with the question whether unlawfully residing aliens could enjoy under the RESC the right to medical assistance and the right of children and young persons to social protection.[39] Interestingly enough, the explicit exclusion of unlawfully residing foreigners in the Appendix of the RESC was for the Committee no reason to not confer a right to them. In more detail, the claimant contested a new French law which provided for only medical treatment and cost coverage in emergencies and life threatening situations for unlawfully staying foreigners. Only unlawfully staying foreigners who could establish three month continuous residence in France and could meet a means test were granted a basic health insurance. The European Committee decided that the Charter, including its Appendix, must be interpreted in the light of its objective and purpose. And when determining this objective and purpose it must be taken into account that the Charter is a living human rights instrument dedicated, most notably, to human dignity and closely complementing the European Convention on Human Rights. The Committee continues that the present case concerns the right to life itself and thus human dignity. Therefore, when interpreting the Appendix, denying the right to medical assistance to illegal foreigners is contrary to the Charter. In this concrete French case, the Committee found no violation of the right to medical assistance (Article 13), because France provides for emergency medical treatment. But this statement only referred to adults. With regard to the right of children, the Committee found an infringement

---

37 European Committee of Social Rights, *Social protection in the European Social Charter: Study compiled on the basis of the case law of the European Committee of Social Rights*, Social Charter Monographs No. 7 (Strasbourg: Council of Europe, 2000), 79.

38 See European Committee of Social Rights, *European Social Charter: Conclusions XIII-4*, by Suzanne Grevisse (Strasbourg: Council of Europe, 1996), 62.

39 European Committee of Social Rights, Decision of 8 September 2004, *FIDH v. France*, Collective Complaint No. 14/2003.

of Article 17 RESC (right of children and young persons to medical assistance) read together with Article E (non-discrimination). This was argued in the decision by referring to the UN Child Rights Convention and stating that children should receive more than just emergency medical treatment. It is interesting to remark that from the report transmitted from the European Committee of Social Rights to the Committee of Ministers it becomes clear that one of the main reasons for reaching this conclusion was the fact that children following their parents cannot be blamed for not having the required permits.[40]

To my mind, there are good reasons to consider it a desirable result that children irrespective of their immigration status are entitled to more than just medical treatment in cases of emergency. Yet the way chosen to reach this result was legally not correct. The relevant provision in the Charter and the Appendix to the Charter are clear and unambiguous: these rights do not apply to foreigners unlawfully present in a contracting state. What else could the drafting state parties have written in the Charter in order to make it clearer? And how can states which want to respect the RESC any longer trust the wording of this document? In my opinion, the RESC does not allow for this conclusion. The Child Rights Convention, by contrast, would do so. Of course, the CRC does not allow for individual or collective complaints. But it would have been an option to challenge the law before national courts by invoking the CRC. There are enough examples where this has been done. Yet, to my knowledge, in this concrete case this did not happen. Anyway, it will be interesting to see how the European Committee of Social Rights will decide in a pending case: an international non-governmental organisation has claimed that the Netherlands violate the RESC by not granting certain forms of social assistance to unlawfully residing children. The complaint has been declared admissible, but so far no decision on the merits has been issued.[41]

The second main human rights instrument of the Council of Europe is the European Convention on Human Rights.[42] This document does not include social rights. Nevertheless, this has not prevented the European Court of Human Rights, which supervises compliance with the Convention, to regard certain aspect of social security as being protected by the Convention. Most notably, the Court nowadays considers an individual's legal position in social security law as ownership; and a disproportionate interference as violation of the right to

40 The report itself is not published. But see Matti Mikkola, "Social human rights of migrants under the European Social Charter," *European Journal of Social Security* 1 (2008): 56, 57.

41 See European Committee of Social Rights, Decision on admissibility of 23 September 2008, *DCI v. The Netherlands*, Collective Complaint No. 47/2008.

42 Convention for the Protection of Human Rights and Fundamental Freedoms, 4 November 1950, ETS No. 005.

property – which is laid down in Article 1 of the First Additional Protocol.[43] Also the right to family life (Article 8) has gained some importance when it has been about access to child benefits. Moreover, the right to life (Article 2) and the prohibition of inhuman and degrading treatment (Article 3) have proven to entail some implications for health care.[44]

The European Convention on Human Rights grants the rights set forth in the Convention to everyone within the jurisdiction of a contracting state. Whether this includes migrants with an irregular status of stay or work in matters of social security will be shortly discussed in the following section.

In a few cases the European Court of Human Rights was confronted with claims of individuals with medical problems who were unlawfully residing in contracting states and faced imminent expulsion. They alleged, most notably, that their repatriation would lead to inhuman and degrading treatment and would be a threat to their life. Due to their bad state of health, the claimants received health care from the contracting states. Such (adequate) health care and medication was difficult or in some cases even impossible to obtain in the countries of origin. Therefore, according to the claimants, an expulsion coming along with an abrupt stop of medical treatment would have led to a serious deterioration of the status of health. The Court had to decide whether aliens who are subject to expulsion can claim any entitlement to remain in the territory of a contracting state in order to continue to benefit from medical assistance. The European Court of Human Rights has just once found the threat of inhuman and degrading treatment and hence a violation of the Convention's guarantees. This was in 1997 in the case *D. v. United Kingdom*.[45] It dealt with an irregular migrant who was terminally ill and had a very poor prognosis already based on the therapy in the United Kingdom. It was estimated that the withdrawal of the current treatment would reduce the prognosis by half. Therefore, the Court found that the implementation of the decision of expulsion would expose the applicant to a real risk of dying under most distressing circumstances. However, the Court stated clearly that the circumstances of this case were very exceptional and that, in principle, no right to remain in the territory of a contracting state can be obtained in order to continue

43 For an analysis of the discussion whether the right to property can be invoked in social security matters see Klaus Kapuy, "Social security and the European Convention on Human Rights: How an odd couple has become presentable," *European Journal of Social Security* 3 (2007): 225 et seq.

44 For an overview of the European Court of Human Rights case law as to social security see Klaus Kapuy, Danny Pieters and Bernhard Zaglmayer, *Social security cases in Europe: The European Court of Human Rights*, Antwerp/Oxford: Intersentia, 2007.

45 European Court of Human Rights, Judgment of 2 May 1997, *D. v. United Kingdom*, Application No. 30240/96.

to benefit from medical, social or other forms of assistance provided by the expelling state.[46] And indeed, this was the first and also the last time that the Court found such exceptional circumstances. So, it seems that the prohibition of inhuman and degrading treatment and also the right to life can only be invoked by irregular migrant workers under extreme, life threatening conditions.

Besides this legal case, there has been no other case where the European Court of Human Rights found in favour of an irregular migrant in the context of social security.

Let me nevertheless point to three other cases which involved legally residing foreigners. Maybe this could also have implications for irregular ones.

In two of them, *Gaygusuz v. Austria*[47] and *Koua Poirrez v. France*[48], the Court found a violation of the principle of non-discrimination based on citizenship read together with the right to property. In the *Gaygusuz* case it was about the entitlement to an emergency assistance which was somehow linked to premium payment. The claimant paid contributions, but was refused this benefit due to a lack of Austrian citizenship. And in *Koua Poirrez* the applicant was denied access to social assistance for disabled adults; also based on the ground that he lacked French citizenship.

In the third case, *Niedzwiecki v. Germany* and *Okpisz v. Germany*, there was an infringement of the principle of non-discrimination based on immigration status read together with the right to family life.[49] The applicants' families were only issued with regularly renewable residence titles for exceptional purposes which did not entitle them to child benefits. Foreigners with stable residence permits, by contrast, could receive such child benefits.

Is it conceivable that irregular migrant workers could in future also rely on discrimination based on citizenship or immigration status under the Convention, when they satisfy all other eligibility requirements for social insurance or social assistance benefits? In my opinion it is certainly not impossible. But the possibility that the Court will follow such an argumentation seems to be rather low. This has to do with the fact that according to the Court's case law, a distinction is

46 *Ibid.*, § 54.

47 European Court of Human Rights, Judgment of 16 September 1996, *Gaygusuz v. Austria*, Application No. 17371/90.

48 European Court of Human Rights, Judgment of 30 September 2003, *Koua Poirrez v. France*, Application No. 40892/98.

49 European Court of Human Rights, Judgments of 25 October 2005, *Niedzwiecki v. Germany*, Application No. 58453/00 and *Okpisz v. Germany*, Application No. 59140/00.

discriminatory if it has no objective and reasonable justification. This was exactly what was found in *Gaygusuz*, *Koua Poirrez*, *Niedzwiecki* and *Okpisz*. But there is still a big difference between lawfully and unlawfully residing foreigners. As regards the latter, state parties to the Convention could bring forward many more arguments why exclusion is objectively and reasonably justified. And moreover in its *Gaygusuz* and *Koua Poirrez* judgments the Court emphasised the fact that the applicants resided lawfully in the contracting state.[50]

Finally, I would like to make a small remark concerning Protocol No. 12 to the European Convention on Human Rights. This Additional Protocol, which is currently in force for 17 Council of Europe Member States, prohibits discrimination not only in conjunction with the rights set forth in the Convention, but in general. Nevertheless, I do not think that this will have more implications for the social security of irregular migrant workers, compared to the 'old' non-discrimination protection under the Convention. The Explanatory Report to Additional Protocol No. 12 makes clear that the non-discrimination assessment will be the same as the assessment under the 'old' non-discrimination provision.[51] With the only difference that also rights not enumerated in the Convention are protected. But social security, to a large extent, is already covered through the right to property.

3. TREATIES ON THE LEGAL STATUS OF MIGRANT WORKERS

This chapter deals with multilateral treaties which address the legal status of migrant workers. These treaties are often considered as human rights treaties particularly for migrant workers. Yet, as will be shown, some of them do not only provide for rights, but also aim to prevent and eliminate irregular migration and work.

3.1. UNIVERSAL LEVEL

The International Labour Organization (ILO) has adopted two Conventions, accompanied by two Recommendations, particularly dealing with the issue of migrant workers. As for the contents, one can see that the first Convention, i.e. Migration for Employment Convention (Revised) No. 97 of 1949, focuses on the

50 See European Court of Human Rights, Judgment of 16 September 1996, *Gaygusuz v. Austria*, Application No. 17371/90, § 46 and Judgment of 30 September 2003, *Koua Poirrez v. France*, Application No. 40892/98, § 47.

51 See Explanatory Report to Protocol No. 12 to the Convention for the Protection of Human Rights and Fundamental Freedoms. Available at http://conventions.coe.int/Treaty/EN/Reports/Html/177.htm.

organisation and facilitation of migrant work.[52] At its core there is a non-discrimination provision for migrants compared to nationals. The latter convention, i.e. Migrant Workers (Supplementary Provisions) Convention No. 143 of 1975, is concerned with, on the one hand, the fight against irregular migration and employment and, on the other hand, the equality of opportunity and treatment for migrant workers.[53] These two objectives are reflected in the structure of the Convention, which is divided into two parts.

Both Conventions leave no doubt that a distinction has to be made between regular and irregular migrant workers. For the purpose of the 1949 Convention and Part Two of the 1975 Convention, which deals with equality of opportunity and treatment for migrant workers, the term migrant worker only includes persons regularly admitted as a migrant for employment.[54] Unlawfully staying and unlawfully working individuals are thus excluded from the scope of protection. By contrast, Part One of the 1975 Convention which is titled 'Migrations in abusive conditions', directly addresses irregular migration and work. This is mostly for the purpose of preventing and suppressing it. Nevertheless, Part One also confers rights to irregular migrant workers. Article 1 of the Convention requires each state party to respect the basic human rights of all migrant workers. But what are the basic human rights granted to every migrant worker regardless of his or her immigration status? The Committee of Experts considers them as the most fundamental human rights, such as the right to life or the right to protection against torture or inhuman or degrading treatment.[55] There is no direct reference made to rights such as the right to social security or the right to health. Indirectly, as we have seen from the case law of the European Court of Human Rights, also such fundamental human rights can have implications when it is about medical treatment in immediate life threatening situations. However, the value of these basic human rights for a person's social security is rather restricted.

Another provision of Part One of Convention No. 143 dealing with rights of irregular migrant workers is Article 9(1). It states that an irregular migrant worker should enjoy equal treatment for himself and his family with regular migrant

---

52 Convention concerning Migration for Employment (Revised), 1 July 1949, Convention No. 097.

53 Convention concerning Migrations in Abusive Conditions and the Promotion of Equality of Opportunity and Treatment of Migrant Workers, 24 June 1975, Convention No. 143.

54 See § 11 (1) C97 and § 11 (1) C143.

55 See International Labour Conference, 66th session, 1980, Report of the Committee of Experts on the Application of Conventions and Recommendations. *General Survey of the Reports relating to Conventions Nos. 97 and 143 and Recommendations Nos. 86 and 151 concerning migrant workers* (Geneva: International Labour Office, 1980), § 257.

workers "in respect of rights arising out of past employment" as regards, most notably, remuneration and social security.[56] This provision intends to protect irregular migrant workers from losing wages and social security benefits from employment actually performed. The question is whether national law which makes social security benefits conditional upon a lawful residence and upon a lawful status of work would be in contradiction to Article 9(1) C143. Such legislation exists in a number of countries.[57] This has also been recognised by the Committee of Experts. The Committee's response was that such conditions "would deprive Article 9(1) of its principal effect".[58] And indeed, one can argue that it is exactly the aim of Article 9(1) C143 to treat irregular and regular migrant workers equally as regards rights arising out of past employment. So, if an irregular migrant worker fulfils all other qualifying conditions, except for the one on regular work or stay, he or she should be treated equally with a regular migrant worker. On the other hand, one can also argue that Article 9(1) C143 explicitly refers to "rights arising out of past employment". So there is the precondition that rights already have been built up/have arisen. If national legislation explicitly denies this, then, according to the wording, there is nothing to be protected by Article 9(1) C143. However, this question remains unsolved. Not least since the Committee of Experts is just a supervisory body, but without competence to interpret the ILO Conventions.[59]

What should also be mentioned in this context is Migrant Workers Recommendation No. 151.[60] Although not legally binding, this Recommendation further specifies the 1975 ILO Convention No. 143. Subsection 34(1)(b) of the Recommendation advises that migrants who leave the country, irrespective of the legality of the stay therein, should be entitled to benefits which may be due in respect of any employment injury suffered. Here it is about the export of benefits to which a worker has already become entitled to. The Committee of Experts has not considered this as establishing an original right to employment injury benefits – which is in my humble opinion a correct conclusion.[61]

---

56 See for the reference group regular migrant workers: *ibid.*, § 260.

57 See for instance France or the Netherlands.

58 See International Labour Conference, 87th session, 1999, Report of the Committee of Experts on the Application of Conventions and Recommendations. *General Survey of the Reports relating to Conventions Nos. 97 and 143 and Recommendations Nos. 86 and 151 concerning migrant workers* (Geneva: International Labour Office, 1999), § 307.

59 See, amongst others, Angelika Nußberger, "Interpretation of international social security standards: Problems and prospects," in *International social security standards: Current views and interpretation matters*, ed. Frans Pennings (Antwerp/Oxford: Intersentia, 2007), 47.

60 Migrant Workers Recommendation, 24 June 1975, Recommendation No. 151.

61 See International Labour Conference, *General Survey concerning migrant workers*, 1999, § 562.

A further recommendation to be mentioned emerges in subsection 34(1)(c)(ii). It reads that migrant workers who leave the country, irrespective of the legality of the stay therein, should be entitled

> "in accordance with national practice, to reimbursement of any social security contributions which have not given and will not give rise to rights under national laws or regulations or international arrangements: Provided that where social security contributions do not permit entitlement to benefits, every effort should be made with a view to the conclusion of bilateral or multilateral agreements to protect the rights of migrants."

In some countries, irregular migrant workers can *de facto* contribute to social security.[62] Admittedly, the possibilities of irregular migrant workers to pay into the social security system are rather limited; but they exist. And once it takes place, such a situation would fall within the ambit of subsection 34(1)(c)(ii) Recommendation No. 151. However, reimbursement of contribution under this Recommendation shall only happen when this is in accordance with national practice. But examples of countries which provide for premium refunding are rather rare. Therefore the impact of this advice will be rather low – see also below.

The third migrant workers treaty at the universal level to be discussed in this work is the UN Convention on the Protection of All Migrant Workers and Members of Their Families (ICMW).[63] This is the most recent treaty and dates from 1990. The objective was ambitious: to bring about the international protection of the rights of *all* migrant workers and their families.[64] In this approach, however, a clear distinction is made between the rights for all migrant workers, including irregular ones, on the one hand, and the rights for only regular migrant workers on the other hand. Moreover, there is also a set of provisions which does not deal with rights, but with measures to prevent and eliminate irregular migration and work. So, for irregular migrant workers we have a situation like in the 1975 ILO Migrant Workers Convention. Rights on the one hand and measures against the phenomenon on the other. Yet the difference between those two conventions is that the UN Convention elaborates in detail what these human rights are; whereas the ILO Convention just stipulates that irregular migrant workers have basic human rights.

---

62 This is for instance the case under the Social Security and Medicare programs in the United States. See, amongst others, Eduardo Porter, "Illegal immigrants are bolstering social security with billions," *New York Times*, 5 April 2005, page A1 or Miriam Jordan, "Even workers in U.S. illegally pay tax man," *Wall Street Journal*, 4 April 2007, page B1.

63 International Convention on the Protection of the Rights of All Migrant Workers and Members of Their Families, UN General Assembly resolution 45/158, 18 December 1990.

64 See Preamble to the UN Migrant Workers Convention.

What are the rights of irregular migrant workers as regards social security under the UN Convention? Two provisions seem to be of particular relevance: Articles 27 and 28 ICMW. Article 27(1) stipulates that

> "[w]ith respect to social security, migrant workers and members of their families shall enjoy in the State of employment the same treatment granted to nationals in so far as they fulfil the requirements provided for by the applicable legislation of that State and the applicable bilateral and multilateral treaties. The competent authorities of the State of origin and the State of employment can at any time establish the necessary arrangements to determine the modalities of application of this norm."

And paragraph 2 continues:

> "Where the applicable legislation does not allow migrant workers and members of their families a benefit, the States concerned shall examine the possibility of reimbursing interested persons the amount of contributions made by them with respect to that benefit on the basis of the treatment granted to nationals who are in similar circumstances."

The value of the first paragraph of this provision for irregular migrant workers is not very clear. Basically, it is a principle for state parties to treat migrant workers, including irregular ones, equally with nationals in social security. But this only insofar as migrant workers fulfil the necessary national and international requirements. Does this mean that if a state party makes social security benefits subject to a regular status of stay or work, this is prohibited under this provision? Or does such a requirement still fall under the competence of the state party? Commentators have thus far not provided a clear answer to the meaning of this provision.[65] *Michael Hasenau*, who is one of the few who takes a clear point of view, argues that Article 27(1) ICMW does not preclude state parties from excluding irregular migrant workers from social security. He bases this position on two arguments: first, the provision leaves the determination of qualifying conditions for social security benefits to state parties, except for discrimination on the ground of nationality. And second, the first draft of the Convention included in Article 27(1) ICMW the phrase "who are documented or are in a regular situation".[66] Both arguments are to my mind not convincing. Whatever

65 See, most notably, Ryszard Cholewinski, *Migrant workers in international human rights law: Their protection in countries of employment* (Oxford: Clarendon Press, 1997), 165, 166; Dirk Vanheule, Marie-Claire Foblets, Sander Loones and Steven Bouckaert, "De betekenis van de V.N.-Arbeidsmigrantenconventie van 18 december 1990 in het geval van ratificatie door België," in *Journal des tribunaux du travail* 894 (2004): 355.

66 Michael Hasenau, "Setting norms in the United Nations System: The Draft Convention on the Protection of the Rights of All Migrant Workers and their Families in Relation to ILO in standards on migrant workers," *International Migration* 2 (1990): 143.

the first draft of this Convention was like, in the final document Article 27(1) is part of Part Three, which grants the rights to all migrant workers and their family members, irrespective of their immigration status. And also the ground of nationality could, under certain circumstances, be invoked by an irregular migrant worker to compare his or her situation with the one of a national. But *Hasenau* is right when he points to the wide margin of appreciation that is granted to contracting states to determine the qualifying conditions for social security coverage. And this brings us back to the initial question: what is then the meaning of this provision for irregular migrant workers? This question is still to be answered by the Committee on the Protection of the Rights of All Migrant Workers and Members of Their Families.

The second paragraph of Article 27 ICMW is about refunding of social security premiums. It reminds us of the Recommendation to the 1975 ILO Migrant Workers Convention. Also there it was recommended that migrant workers should get their social security contributions reimbursed if, first, the contributions have not given and will not give rise to rights and, second, if reimbursement is in accordance with national practice. Here, under the UN Convention, reimbursement should be considered if, first, migrant workers are not eligible for benefits and, second, nationals in similar circumstances can get a refund. The two provisions seem to resemble each other. But when it comes to irregular workers, there might be a difference. That is to say, when there is a reimbursement scheme in place for foreigners, but not for nationals. Let me give an example. The Swiss General Old Age and Surviving Dependant's Pensions Act provides for contribution refund for non-citizens who are not covered by bilateral social security agreements.[67] Imagine that it would be possible for irregular migrant workers to contribute to the Swiss old age and survivors' pension. Then, according to the ILO Recommendation, these irregular migrant workers should be able to recover their contributions, because reimbursement is in accordance with national practice. On the other hand, pursuant to the UN Migrant Workers Convention, migrant workers shall only be able to get their premiums refunded on the basis of the treatment which is granted to nationals who are in similar circumstances. But nationals cannot get their premiums reimbursed. They instead receive their benefits. So, since Article 27(2) ICMW is to be read as a non-discrimination provision, irregular migrant workers fall outside its protection, whenever there is no reimbursement scheme for nationals. In this regard the 1990 UN Convention provides less protection than the 1975 ILO Recommendation. However, it must be borne in mind that the ILO Recommendation is in contrast to the UN Convention

67 See Gijsbert Vonk and Klaus Kapuy, "Three approaches to refunding social insurance contributions to temporary migrant workers: Is there an attractive policy alternative?" in *European Journal of Social Security* 3 (2008): 228, 236.

not legally binding. In addition, it must be recalled that the practical impact of both premium reimbursement provisions will be rather low. This is so, because examples of premium refund are scarce in national legislation.

The second provision under the ICMW, which is of particular relevance for irregular migrant workers, is Article 28. It reads as follows:

> "Migrant workers and members of their families shall have the right to receive any medical care that is urgently required for the preservation of their life or the avoidance of irreparable harm to their health on the basis of equality of treatment with nationals of the State concerned. Such emergency medical care shall not be refused them by reason of any irregularity with regard to stay or employment."

This article establishes a clear entitlement to emergency medical care for irregular migrant workers and their family members. As illustrated before, in 2008 General Comment No. 19 on the ICESCR's right to social security was published. According to the Committee on Economic, Social and Cultural Rights, the right to social security under the ICESCR includes primary and emergency medical care for all persons irrespective of their immigration status. So there is a tendency to provide for more than emergency medical treatment. Still, this has been an interpretation of the ICESCR. Here, in the UN Migrant Workers Convention, by contrast, this entitlement is written in the law itself.

Linda Bosniak has pointed, in the context of the right to emergency medical care, to a serious weakness of the UN Migrant Workers Convention: there is no protection for irregular migrant workers to actually exercise their rights.[68] There is nothing which would preclude that health care providers inform or are obliged to inform immigration authorities about a patient with an irregular immigration status. Such a lack of guarantees could deter irregular migrant workers in practice from exercising their rights.

Finally, it must be noted that in Part Four of the ICMW, which applies to migrant workers in a regular situation only, one can find the principle of equal treatment in relation to access to health services between migrant workers and their family members on the one hand and nationals of the state of employment on the other hand. This principle is subject to the condition that the regular migrant worker and his or her family members fulfil the requirements for participation in the

---

68 See Linda Bosniak, "Human rights, state sovereignty and the protection of undocumented migrants under the international Migrant Workers' Convention," in *Irregular migration and human rights: Theoretical, European and international perspectives*, ed. Barbara Bogusz, Ryszard Cholewinski, Adam Cygan and Erika Szyszczak (Leiden/Boston: Martinus Nijhoff Publishers, 2004), 336, 337.

respective national schemes.[69] Nevertheless, it is an obligation to not discriminate, which does not apply to migrant workers in an irregular situation.

3.2. EUROPEAN LEVEL

In Europe, the Council of Europe adopted in 1977 the European Convention on the Legal Status of Migrant Workers.[70] This Convention sets out minimum obligations of the state parties regarding the legal status of migrant workers. Amongst these obligations, there is the duty not to discriminate migrant workers against national workers in the field of social security. However, irregular migrant workers are explicitly excluded from the personal scope of application of the whole Convention. Article 1(1) stipulates that "for the purpose of this Convention, the term 'migrant worker' shall mean a national of a Contracting Party who has been authorised by another Contracting Party to reside in its territory in order to take up paid employment".

To sum up, it is striking that two of the four instruments on the legal status of migrant workers completely exclude irregular migrant workers from their scope of application. These are the two instruments which just contain rights for migrant workers. The other two treaties, by contrast, comprise both rights and measures against irregular migration and work. And they do also confer rights to irregular migrant workers. So it seems that there is just a consensus for granting rights to migrants with an irregular immigration status, when at the same time the fight against this phenomenon is emphasised.

What are the rights to be conferred to irregular migrant workers under these treaties? Without doubt, there is the right to emergency medical care. Then we can find the principle of equal treatment between all migrant workers, including irregular ones, and nationals in social security; and the principle of equal treatment between irregular migrant workers and regular ones in respect of rights arising out of past employment. To what extent state parties are confined by these principles in their rights to link benefit entitlement to a lawful stay or lawful work is somewhat vague. And finally, premium reimbursement should be considered by the contracting state. This is of course subject to previous premium payment by irregular migrant workers; and subject to national practice in general or practice regarding nationals.

69 See § 43 (1) (e) and § 45 (1) (c) ICMW.

70 European Convention on the Legal Status of Migrant Workers, 24 November 1977, ETS No. 093.

It is important to mention that the migrant worker treaties have a rather poor status of ratification. This is in particular true for the Council of Europe's Migrant Worker Convention, which has so far eleven ratifications, and the 1975 ILO Convention C143 with 23 ratifications. The 1990 UN Migrant Workers Convention has 41 ratifications – but these ratifications are almost exclusively from migrant sending countries.

4. SOCIAL SECURITY STANDARD SETTING TREATIES

So far this analysis has dealt with instruments which provide for human rights and migrant workers rights and analysed their impact on the social security of irregular migrant workers. In this chapter multilateral instruments which further develop the contents of the right to social security will be analysed. These are the standard setting treaties of the International Labour Organization (ILO) and the Council of Europe (CoE). They prescribe the minimum percentage of workers or of the population to be protected, the conditions for entitlement, the duration of benefit payment and the minimum rate of benefits. The basic instrument is the ILO Social Security (Minimum Standards) Convention 102 from 1952, covering all branches of social security.[71] Subsequently, further conventions have been adopted which set higher standards for particular branches of social security. These are the Conventions 121, 128, 130 and 168.[72] Following the approach taken in ILO Convention 102, the Council of Europe adopted the European Code of Social Security and the Revised European Code of Social Security.[73]

As indicated, it is up to the contracting states to define the scope *ratione materiae* of their social security legislation. These standard conventions only lay down that a certain percentage of the residents, the employees or the economically active population must be covered. It would, nevertheless, be interesting to know whether irregular migrant workers must be taken into consideration when calculating the percentage. This is, unfortunately, not clear. There is no explicit reference made to this group. And also the definitions of terms, such as residents,

---

71 Convention concerning Minimum Standards of Social Security, 28 June 1952, Convention No. 102.

72 Convention concerning Benefits in the Case of Employment Injury, 8 July 1964, Convention No. 121; Convention concerning Invalidity, Old-Age and Survivors' Benefits, 29 June 1967, Convention No. 128; Convention concerning Medical Care and Sickness Benefits, 25 June 1969, Convention No. 130; Convention concerning Employment Promotion and Protection against Unemployment, 21 June 1988, Convention No. 168.

73 European Code of Social Security, 16 April 1964, ETS No. 048 and European Code of Social Security (Revised), 6 November 1990, ETS No. 139.

do not give more information. Residents are under all of these conventions defined as persons ordinarily resident in the territory of the contracting state. But ordinary resident can mean both: legally and illegally residing. Also a look at the ILO Constitution does not provide information. Only the original, the old ILO Constitution of 1919 stated in Article 41, point 8 that "the standard set by law in each country with respect to the conditions of labour should have due regard to the equitable economic treatment of all workers lawfully resident therein".[74] Yet this constitution is outdated. And also the Statute of the Council of Europe is silent on this issue. Interpretation of these terms which would shed light on the situation of irregular residents has not been given.

Besides determining minimum coverage, most of these conventions also contain a principle of non-discrimination. Convention 121 states in Article 27 that a state party "shall within is territory assure to non-nationals equality of treatment with its own nationals as regards employment injury benefits". Similarly, Article 32 of Convention 130 stipulates that each state party "shall, within its territory, assure to non-nationals who normally reside or work there equality of treatment with its own nationals as regards the right to the benefits provided for in this Convention." The first cited non-discrimination provision leaves it completely open which immigration status a foreign worker must have. The latter provision talks about normally residing. But also this concept is not clearly defined and could also be understood to include unlawfully residing persons.

Interesting is the non-discrimination provision in flagship Convention 102 on social security minimum standards. Article 68 also requires state parties to grant non-national residents the same rights as national residents. But at the same time it allows for exceptions. If the benefits or portions of the benefits are paid whole or mainly out of public funds, then special rules for non-nationals may be applied. Moreover, under contributory social security schemes for employees, equality of treatment may be made subject to the existence of bilateral or multilateral agreements providing for reciprocity. This leaves state parties a quite large margin of appreciation, not only with regard to irregular migrant workers. In reciprocity agreements it is completely up to the states to decide whether they include or exclude irregular migrants. And also regarding public funded benefits, the way for special provisions and therefore also for exclusion of irregular migrants is paved.

---

74 Constitution of the International Labour Organization, adopted by the Peace Conference in April 1919. The Constitution became Part XIII of the Treaty of Versailles (28 June 1919). See Article 427 point 8 Treaty of Versailles: available at http://net.lib.byu.edu/~rdh7/wwi/versa/versa13.html.

So, concerning the status of irregular migrant workers under social security standard setting treaties, it can be observed that this group is not recognised as a special group. There is no reference made to them in the instruments itself, but also not in the scarce interpretation. This brings us to the deeper problem. The only body which is authorised to interpret the ILO conventions is the International Court of Justice. But this Court has never done so. The International Labour Office and the Committee of Experts have no authority for interpretation.[75] In fact, of course, they provide a form of guidance. But even this guidance sheds no light on the questions posed in this work.

5. EUROPEAN UNION LAW

Irregular migration has played a prominent role in the European Union (EU) policy of the last decade. The basis for this focus has been the Treaty of Amsterdam in 1997, which gave the Union more far-reaching competences in the field of asylum and immigration. Up till then the Member States only cooperated in an intergovernmental way in this area. Since the incorporation of the Treaty of Amsterdam into the EC-Treaty, Article 63(3)(b) EC-Treaty has provided for taking measures in the field of illegal immigration and illegal residence. This competence basically leaves open which measures are to be adopted. The following years, however, have demonstrated that the activities in the field of illegal immigration and illegal residence were of a rather restrictive nature. *Ryszard Cholewinski* has called this a 'security approach'[76], meaning that it has been the fight against illegal immigration, not the protection of the rights of irregular migrants, which was at the centre of the Union's illegal migration policy. To name a few of the legally binding measures, which have been taken to combat illegal migration into the European Union:

- Directive 2001/40 on the mutual recognition of decisions on the expulsion of third-country nationals;
- Directive 2002/90 defining the facilitation on unauthorised entry, transit and residence;
- Framework Decision 2002/926 on combating trafficking in human beings;

75 See, amongst others, Angelika Nußberger, "Interpretation of international social security standards: Problems and prospects," in *International social security standards: Current views and interpretation matters*, ed. Frans Pennings (Antwerp/Oxford: Intersentia, 2007), 46, 47.

76 Ryszard Cholewinski, "European Union policy on irregular migration: Human rights lost?" in *Irregular migration and human rights: Theoretical, European and international perspectives*, ed. Barbara Bogusz, Ryszard Cholewinski, Adam Cygan and Erika Szyszczak (Leiden/Boston: Martinus Nijhoff Publishers, 2004), 182.

- Framework Decision 2002/946 on the strengthening of the penal framework to prevent the facilitation of unauthorised entry, transit and residence;
- Directive 2003/110 on assistance in cases of transit for the purposes of removal by air;
- Directive 2008/115 on common standards and procedures in Member States for returning illegally staying third-country nationals; or
- a number of readmission agreements.

The most recent measure to be adopted is a Directive providing for sanctions against employers of illegally staying third-country nationals. This Directive has already passed the European Parliament, but must still be formally approved by the Council.

The latest EC law in the fight against illegal migration, i.e. above cited Directive 2008/115 from December 2008, differs in one regard from the other measures: here we can find safeguards on health during periods of voluntary departure and during periods for which removal has been postponed. Therefore, this Directive will be analysed in this chapter.

In contrast to the fight against irregular migration, little has been done with the explicit aim to protect irregular migrants. The most noteworthy legally binding document is Directive 2004/81 on the residence permit issued to third-country nationals who are victims of trafficking in human beings. Accordingly, also this Directive will be investigated in this chapter.

But not only third-country nationals can work and stay unlawfully in an EU Member State. Also citizens of one EU Member State can do so in another EU Member State. In more detail, citizens of the EU-15 Member States basically have the right to take up employment in another Member State and, based on this employment, to reside there. So, if no exceptional circumstances apply, they cannot be irregular migrant workers in an EU country. Almost the same can as of 1 May 2009 be said about citizens of those ten countries which entered the EU in 2004. Then the remaining restrictions on the free movement of workers are lifted in the vast majority of the old Member States.[77] In 2007, Bulgaria and Romania entered the EU. Also for those countries the transitional arrangements in the Accession Treaties provide for restrictions on the free movement of workers. Here, eleven out of 25 Member States still close their labour markets (leaving here aside the free movement of services). In these Member States, Bulgarian and Romanian workers can work irregularly. So to sum up, there are citizens of a few EU-Member States which can work irregularly in a few other Member States.

77 The restrictions on the free movement of workers only continue to apply in Austria and Germany.

I will first have a look at Regulation 1612/68 on freedom of movement for workers within the Community. This Regulation provides for equal treatment between citizens of EU Member States with regard to social advantages.

5.1. EC REGULATION 1612/68

Regulation 1612/68 aims to facilitate the freedom of movement for workers within the Community. A central provision of the Regulation is Article 7.[78] It states:

> " 1. A worker who is a national of a Member State may not, in the territory of another Member State, be treated differently from national workers by reason of his nationality in respect of any conditions of employment and work, in particular as regards remuneration, dismissal, and should he become unemployed, reinstatement or re-employment;
> 2. He shall enjoy the same social and tax advantages as national workers."

For our investigation it is relevant to ask whether a worker from one of the new Member States who works illegally in another Member State may also fall back on this non-discrimination provision and, consequently, enjoy the same social advantages as national workers.

The transitional arrangements in the Accession Treaties do not provide for restrictions of Article 7(2) Regulation 1612/68. Therefore, this provision is in its entirety applicable to citizens of the new Member States.

The definition of worker under Regulation 1612/68 is linked to Article 39 of the EC-Treaty. According to settled case law, the concept of worker "has a specific Community meaning and must not be interpreted narrowly".[79] The European Court of Justice (ECJ) ruled that a worker is an individual who for a certain period of time "performs services for and under the direction of another person in return for which he receives remuneration".[80] The Court has additionally established a number of other criteria for meeting the definition of workers, such as for instance that the activities must be real and genuine, and not only marginal and ancillary. None of these criteria, however, relates to the immigration status of the worker.

Therefore, the formal interpretation of the wording would lead to the conclusion that irregular migrant workers shall enjoy the same social advantages as national

78 Regulation (EEC) No 1612/68 of the Council of 15 October 1968 on freedom of movement for workers within the Community, OJ L. 257, 19 October 1968.

79 European Court of Justice, 7 September 2004, C-456/02 (*Trojani*) [2004] ECR I-7573, § 15.

80 *Ibid.*

workers. The ECJ has never been confronted with a legal case like that; this means with a case which enquires whether a citizen from one Member State who works illegally in another Member State shall enjoy the same social advantages as a national worker based on Article 7(2) Regulation 1612/68. The question therefore is what could be the reaction of the ECJ in such a situation. *Herwig Verschueren* suggests that the *Akrich* case could serve as a reference.[81] This case was about family reunification under Article 10 of Regulation 1612/68.[82] In more detail, it dealt with the right of third-country nationals to reunify with an EU national who works in another EU Member State. There the Court ruled that the third-country national "must be lawfully resident in a Member State when he or she moves to another Member State to which the citizen of the Union is migrating or has migrated".[83] But this solution by the ECJ is not completely satisfying, since 'lawful residence' is not explicitly demanded by the Regulation. And moreover, this "prior lawful residence" requirement has been overruled by the Court in the *Metock* case.[84] More elegant, and I agree with *Herwig Verschueren*, is the solution offered by the Advocate General.[85] The Advocate General proposed that the Member State may invoke an overriding national interest and hence refuse the entry of a family member who is a third-country national. The Member State's competence, according to the Advocate General, "stems from the interest in the viability and enforceability of immigration laws".[86] This so-called 'rule of reason' could also be applied to our question. Meaning that citizens of one EU Member State who work in contradiction to national immigration laws in another EU Member State, could be prevented from enjoying the same social advantages as a national worker by arguing with an overriding national interest. The overriding national interest could be, like in the General Advocate proposed in the *Akrich* case, the viability and enforceability of immigration laws. In particular, it could be the interest to protect the national labour market, which is expressed by a Member State's use of EC-transitional periods for the freedom of movement of workers.

Another reason for not applying the equal treatment principle of Article 7(2) Regulation 1612/68 to irregular migrant workers might be the argument of misuse of Community law. National immigration law, in accordance with EC-legislation,

81 Herwig Verscheuren, "Toegang tot minimumvoorzieningen voor mensen zonder papieren: Een aftasten van de grenzen van het Europees recht," in *Tijdschrift voor sociaal recht* 4 (2005): 758 et seq.
82 European Court of Justice, 23 September 2003, C-109/01 (*Akrich*) [2003] ECR I-9607.
83 *Ibid.*, § 1.
84 European Court of Justice, 25 July 2008, C-127/08 (*Metock*).
85 Opinion of the Advocate General Geelhoed in European Court of Justice, 23 September 2003, C-109/01 (*Akrich*) [2003] ECR I-9607.
86 *Ibid.*, § 186.

does not allow for the employment of citizens of particular EU-countries. This prohibition, often together with the prohibition of residence, may entail that irregular migrant workers are excluded from social security. Recourse to EC equal treatment provisions in order to evade the application of the national legislation and get access to social advantages could be seen as a misuse. The ECJ has developed the concept of misuse of EC law. In the *Emsland-Stärke* case, the ECJ required for the finding of an abuse both an objective and a subjective element.[87] First, there must be "a combination of objective circumstances in which, despite formal observance of the conditions laid down by the Community rules, the purpose of those rules has not been achieved".[88] And second, there must be "a subjective element consisting in the intention to obtain an advantage from the Community rules by creating artificially the conditions laid down for obtaining it".[89] One can see that in contrast to the 'rule of reason' doctrine, the concept of misuse of Community law depends to a much greater extent on the individual circumstance of the case. And in particular the subjective element will cause some difficulties. For our purpose, it is to find that the irregular migrant worker wanted to obtain a social advantage and therefore migrated to another Member State and took up work there. Without excluding this possibility, it seems that most of the time work itself is the driving force.

To conclude, the equal treatment provision with regard to social advantages under Regulation 1612/68 would, according to the wording, be also applicable to irregular migrant workers from the new EU Member States. Whether the ECJ would follow such a formal interpretation may be doubted. In a case dealing with the right of a third-country national to reunify with a migrating EU worker under Regulation 1612/68, the ECJ assumed that the residence must have been lawful, although the wording of the Regulation does not require this. But there would be also other ways for the ECJ to prevent an irregular migrant worker from enjoying social advantages on an equal footing with national workers; such as the application of the 'rule of reason' doctrine or the concept of misuse of Community law. The latter, however, has some shortcomings in general and may in particular not lead to the result that the irregular migrant workers intended to abuse Community law.

---

87 European Court of Justice, 14 December 2000, C-110/99 (*Emsland-Stärke*) [2000] ECR I-11569.

88 *Ibid.*, § 52.

89 *Ibid.*, § 53. This subjective element has lead to somewhat discussion, since the ECJ explicitly ruled on other occasions that the workers motives are irrelevant – see European Court of Justice, 23 March 1982, C-53/81 (*Levin*) [1982] ECR 1035.

5.2. EC DIRECTIVE 2004/81

EC Directive No. 2004/81 aims to provide, most notably, victims of trafficking in human beings, who cooperate with national authorities, with a residence permit for the duration of the relevant national proceedings.[90] The Directive establishes, basically, the conditions for issuing the residence permit and the treatment which should be granted to victims. The Directive is only applicable to third-country nationals. Article 3 explicitly stipulates that, in order to belong to the personal scope of application of this Directive, it does not matter whether these third-country nationals have illegally entered the territory of the Member State. As for the protection, the Directive distinguishes between the treatment which must be granted during the reflection period and the treatment after the issue of a residence permit. The reflection period shall allow the victim to recover and escape the influence of the perpetrator in order to make a decision as to whether he or she wants to cooperate with the competent authorities. Within this period no expulsion shall be possible. Also within this period, Article 7(1) requires Member States to guarantee third-country nationals who do not have sufficient resources a standard of living capable of ensuring their subsistence and access to emergency medical treatment. After the issue of a residence permit, Member States must ensure more social protection. To be more precise, Article 9 stipulates that Member States "shall provide necessary medical or other assistance to the third-country nationals concerned, who do not have sufficient resources and have special needs, such as pregnant women, the disabled or victims of sexual violence or other forms of violence."

This work deals with irregular migrant workers, i.e. migrant workers who work in contradiction to immigration laws and either stay lawfully or unlawfully in the country of work. The provisions of the victims of human trafficking Directive, which grant medical treatment and a sort of social assistance, can also be relevant for irregular migrant workers, since they may also lack sufficient resources and may also be a victim of human trafficking.

We can see that before the issue of a residence permit, victims of human trafficking are only entitled to emergency medical treatment, whereas thereafter they enjoy, under certain circumstances, necessary medical care. So the extent of the right to health care increases with the degree of the stability of the residence status of the third-country national. This is a rather interesting observation. EC law not only

---

90 Council Directive 2004/81/EC of 29 April 2004 on the residence permit issued to third-country nationals who are victims of trafficking in human beings or who have been the subject of an action to facilitate illegal immigration, who cooperate with the competent authorities, OJ L. 261, 6 August 2004.

expressly links the right to medical care to a certain residence status, but it enhances the right as the stability of the residence status increases: a victim of human trafficking per se is not guaranteed any medical treatment; a victim of human trafficking who has come to the attention of public authorities, is given the opportunity to consider cooperation with national authorities and may not be expelled is granted the right to emergency medical treatment; and, finally, a victim of human trafficking who is issued a temporary residence permit is, under certain circumstances, entitled to necessary medical assistance. So in this Directive, EC law clearly follows the logic to enhance the social protection of foreigners to the extent their stability of residence increases.

Besides medical care, victims of human trafficking who do not have sufficient resources must be granted a standard of living capable of ensuring their subsistence. This is granted before the issue of a residence permit and explicitly regardless of the immigration status. What this standard exactly is, is unfortunately not determined. It seems to be a sort of minimum social assistance. The Netherlands, for instance, do not include these victims in their general social assistance scheme (*Wet Werk en Bijstand*). But, by incorporating this EC Directive, they protect victims of human trafficking who cooperate with national authorities under a specific assistance scheme for aliens (*Regeling verstrekkingen bepaalde categorieën vreemdelingen*). There they are entitled to a financial allowance, which is, in contrast to the general social assistance scheme, not linked to 'back to work' efforts.

5.3. EC DIRECTIVE 2008/115

The objective of EC Directive No. 2008/115 is to establish common rules concerning return, removal, use of coercive measures, detention and entry bans for unlawfully staying third-country nationals.[91] The Directive is applicable to all third-country nationals staying illegally on the territory of a Member State. Illegal stay is defined as presence in a Member State without fulfilling the conditions of entry as set out in Article 5 of the Schengen Borders Code or other conditions for entry, stay or residence in that Member State.[92] Member States, however, are entitled to exclude certain illegally staying third-country nationals from the application of this Directive. This relates, for instance, to third-country nationals who are subject to return as a criminal law sanction.[93]

91 Directive 2008/115/EC of the European Parliament and of the Council of 16 December 2008 on common standards and procedures in Member States for returning illegally staying third-country nationals, OJ L. 348, 24 December 2008.

92 See § 2 (1) and § 3 (2) EC Directive 2008/115.

93 See § 2 (2) EC Directive 2008/115.

Concerning the social security of illegally staying third-country nationals, Article 14 of the Directive is of particular relevance. Under the heading 'Safeguards pending return' it reads:

> "1. Member States shall, with the exception of the situation covered in Articles 16 and 17, ensure that the following principles are taken into account as far as possible in relation to third-country nationals during the period for voluntary departure granted in accordance with Article 7 and during periods for which removal has been postponed in accordance with Article 9: [...] (b) emergency health care and essential treatment of illness are provided;
>
> 2. Member States shall provide the persons referred to in paragraph 1 with a written confirmation in accordance with national legislation that the period for voluntary departure has been extended in accordance with Article 7(2) or that the return decision will temporarily not be enforced."

So, basically, Member States shall provide, as far as possible, unlawfully staying third-country nationals during periods for voluntary departure or during periods of postponed removal orders with emergency health care and essential treatment of illness. As for voluntary departure, Article 7 of the Directive stipulates that Member States shall, if there is no profound reason to refrain from it, grant illegally staying third-country nationals an appropriate period for voluntary departure. And as regards the postponement of a removal, Article 9 calls upon Member States to do so whenever the principle of non-refoulement is violated and whenever the review of a return decision has a suspensory effect. Moreover, Member States may consider postponement of removal whenever the circumstances of the individual case demand it; this relates, in particular, to a person's physical or mental state or to technical reasons, such as lack of transport capacity or failure of the removal due to lack of identification.

Emergency health care and essential treatment of illness are not further specified in Directive 2008/115. However, it is striking that exactly the same terms are used as in Directive 2003/9, which lays down minimum standards for the reception of asylum seekers.[94] There, Article 15 stipulates that "Member States shall ensure that applicants receive the necessary health care which shall include, at least, emergency care and essential treatment of illness". Many Member States have implemented the asylum reception Directive as granting asylum seekers the usual basic statutory health insurance package or an equivalent.[95] The question is whether Member States will implement Directive 2008/115 in a similar way. A

94 See Council Directive 2003/9/EC of 27 January 2003 laying down minimum standards for the reception of asylum seekers, OJ L. 31, 6 February 2003.

95 See for instance Austria, Belgium or the Netherlands.

close look at the wording of both Directives reveals that in Directive 2008/115 it is about 'emergency health care and essential treatment of illness', whereas Directive 2003/9 talks about 'necessary health care which shall include, at least, emergency care and essential treatment of illness'. This could indicate that the bottom line for medical care for asylum seekers is a little bit higher than for illegal staying third-country nationals under Directive 2008/115. Moreover, Directive 2003/9 requires that Member States 'shall ensure' this kind of medical treatment, whereas Directive 2008/115 stipulates that Member States 'shall ensure as far as possible' this medical care. So, the protection for illegally staying third-country nationals is formulated in much weaker terms.

Article 14 of Directive 2008/115 rules that the safeguards for pending returns shall not be applicable to situations covered in Articles 16 and 17. These two provisions refer to situations of detention. Nevertheless, Article 16 stipulates that in detention particular attention shall be paid to the situation of vulnerable persons and that emergency health care and essential treatment of illness shall be provided.

As mentioned before, Member States may exclude certain unlawfully staying third-country nationals from the application of this Directive, such as persons who are subject to return as a criminal law sanction. Article 4(4)(a), however, rules that Member States shall ensure that the treatment and level of protection of those excluded persons are no less favourable than as set out in, amongst others, Article 14(1)(b). In other words, emergency health care and essential treatment of illness shall also be ensured as far as possible to those unlawfully staying third-country nationals who are exempted from the application of the Directive by virtue of Article 2(2).

6. CONCLUSIONS

The first conclusion to be drawn is that there is not one international or supranational legal instrument particularly and comprehensively dealing with the social security of irregular migrant workers.

Second, international and supranational legislation which is relevant for an individual's social security generally does not explicitly address irregular migrant workers. And if this group of workers is directly addressed, then it is mostly for the purpose of denying them social security rights or combating illegal migration and illegal work.

What are the social security rights which have been identified in this analysis? Irregular migrant workers are at least entitled to emergency medical treatment. In the view of the Committee on Economic, Social and Cultural Rights, the entitlement should go further. All forms of primary medical care must be provided to this group. And under European Union law, unlawfully staying third-country nationals should be provided, as far as possible, with emergency health care and essential treatment of illness, during periods for voluntary departure or during periods of postponed removal orders. So we can see a tendency in international and supranational law to grant more than just aid in medical emergencies. Moreover, in many national laws in Europe one can already find more far-reaching guarantees. Often, it is medically *necessary* care, which is provided to aliens, irrespective of their immigration status.

In addition, the analysis has shown that particularly vulnerable groups amongst irregular migrants receive more social protection under international and European Community law:

- women migrant workers should have their basic needs fulfilled during pregnancy or maternity (*interpretation, universal*);
- abused women migrant workers should be entitled to social services (*interpretation, universal*);
- victims of human trafficking who cooperate with national authorities are entitled to a standard of living capable of ensuring their subsistence (*law, Europe*); and
- children should receive full social protection (*interpretation, universal*).

In international treaties on the status of migrant workers, we can find the principle of equal treatment between all migrant workers, including irregular ones, and nationals in social security. But since this equal treatment is made subject to the fulfilment of conditions in national social security legislation, it can be doubted whether irregular migrant workers can effectively benefit from this principle. The same uncertainty goes for equal treatment provisions between regular and irregular migrant workers as regards rights arising out of past employment. What seem to be applicable to irregular migrant workers are premium reimbursement provisions under international law. However, as illustrated, the practical relevance of these provisions will be almost zero.

What could be invoked by irregular migrant workers under international law are general non-discrimination provisions. According to the interpretation of these provisions, nationality and also immigration status can be forbidden grounds of discrimination. Nevertheless, as demonstrated in this work, irregular migrant workers are not per se in an analogous situation to nationals or regular migrant workers. And if they are found to be in a comparable situation, there may still be reasons that justify a difference in treatment.

Looking at the development of international law covering the social security of irregular migrant workers, we can see that states have been aware of this issue for a long time. This is demonstrated by the fact that, for instance, ILO Convention 97 of 1949 or the European Social Charter of 1961 explicitly exclude foreigners who have no permission to stay or to work in a country from their personal scope of application. Yet it has been the recent two decades that this issue has attracted most interest. For the first time, international and European committees and courts have expressly dealt with this issue and irregular migrant workers have been afforded some kind of social protection.

This poses two issues to be discussed. First, the contents: is the social protection provided for irregular migrant workers under international and supranational law sufficient? And, second, the form: is the way in which the social security of irregular migrant workers in international and supranational law is laid down adequate?

Concerning the first, this is certainly a difficult question to answer. However, there is a reason why I do not ask if the social protection under international and supranational law is too much, but if it is sufficient. The bottom line is emergency medical treatment which should explicitly be provided. Only particularly vulnerable groups should receive more than that. The right to emergency medical treatment can be derived from the human right to life. A human right to which most countries are legally bound and which is rather undisputed. This, to my mind, justifies enquiring if there should be more, and not less, protection. Nevertheless, an answer to this question would go beyond the scope of this investigation. Still, in this context I want to refer to other research which has already been carried out; most notably the research under the auspices of the Council of Europe by *Cholewinski*, *Pieters* or *Schoukens*.

The second question is whether the way the social security of this group is shaped in international and supranational law is adequate. The presentation has illustrated that human rights law, social security standard setting law and – and this is quite interesting – even law on the legal status of migrant workers is not very clear when it comes to the social security of irregular migrant workers. To a lesser extent this is also true for EU law. But concerning EU law, there are clear competences regarding its interpretation. Moreover, the European Court of Justice has developed a very subtle case law in general, which can serve to solve questions related to the social security of irregular migrant workers. This cannot be said about most of the ILO, UN or CoE law. Therefore, we often have ambiguous legal texts on irregular migrant workers and we have limited possibilities of interpretation. This combination is, as we have seen, often rather dissatisfying. Desirable would be clear statements on the universal and European level in relation to the social security of irregular migrant workers. The question is of course whether such agreements to harmonise standards could be reached. This brings us back to the difficult question of the contents.

Without answering it, I want to remark that there might be an argument why such a clear statement, maybe in the form of a separate treaty on the social security status of irregular migrant workers, must not be a mission impossible. It is about a particular group. Therefore, the status of this group could always be referred to the social security status of other groups. For instance, when it is about irregular migrant workers themselves, there could always be a reference to national workers. When, what will mostly be the case, irregular migrant workers work in the black economy, a reference to citizens who work in the black economy seems to be reasonable. Children of irregular migrant workers could, regardless of their immigration status, be compared to national children. And so on. This, of course, does not completely solve the problem. For instance, does it mean that an irregular migrant worker who works in the black economy should be treated equally to a national worker who does so? Or does it mean that the foreigner should just receive a little bit less protection? But what is this little bit less protection? Still, despite these problems it would make the whole mission a little bit easier.

BIBLIOGRAPHY

Bosniak, Linda. "Human rights, state sovereignty and the protection of undocumented migrants under the international Migrant Workers' Convention." In *Irregular migration and human rights: Theoretical, European and international perspectives*, edited by Barbara Bogusz, Ryszard Cholewinski, Adam Cygan and Erika Szyszczak, 311–341. Leiden/Boston: Martinus Nijhoff Publishers, 2004.

Cholewinski, Ryszard. "European Union policy on irregular migration: Human rights lost?" In *Irregular migration and human rights: Theoretical, European and international perspectives*, edited by Barbara Bogusz, Ryszard Cholewinski, Adam Cygan and Erika Szyszczak, 159–192. Leiden/Boston: Martinus Nijhoff Publishers, 2004.

Cholewinski, Ryszard. *Migrant workers in international human rights law: Their protection in countries of employment*. Oxford: Clarendon Press, 1997.

Committee on Economic, Social and Cultural Rights. *General Comment No. 14: The right to the highest attainable standard of health (Art.12)*. E/C.12/2000/4. New York: United Nations, 2000.

Committee on Economic, Social and Cultural Rights. *General Comment No. 19: The right to social security (Art.9)*. E/C.12/GC/19. New York: United Nations, 2008.

Committee on the Elimination of Discrimination against Women. *General Recommendation No. 26 on women migrant workers*. CEDAW/C/2009/WP.1/R, New York: United Nations, 2008.

Committee on the Elimination of Racial Discrimination. *General Recommendation No. 30: Discrimination against no non citizens*. New York: United Nations, 2005.

Committee on the Rights of the Child. *General Recommendation No. 6: Treatment of unaccompanied and separated children outside their country of origin*. CRC/GC/2005/6, New York: United Nations, 2005.

European Committee of Social Rights. *European Social Charter: Conclusions XIII-4*. By Suzanne Grevisse. Strasbourg: Council of Europe, 1996.

European Committee of Social Rights. *Social protection in the European Social Charter: Study compiled on the basis of the case law of the European Committee of Social Rights*. Social Charter Monographs No. 7. Strasbourg: Council of Europe, 2000.

Hasenau, Michael. "Setting norms in the United Nations System: The Draft Convention on the Protection of the Rights of All Migrant Workers and their Families in Relation to ILO in standards on migrant workers." *International Migration* 2 (1990): 133–157.

Human Rights Committee. *General Comment No. 15: The position of aliens under the Covenant*, in compilation of General Comments and General Recommendations adopted by Human Rights Treaty Bodies. UN Doc HRI/GEN/1/Rev.8. New York: United Nations, 2006.

International Labour Conference. 66th session, 1980. Report of the Committee of Experts on the Application of Conventions and Recommendations. *General Survey of the Reports relating to Conventions Nos. 97 and 143 and Recommendations Nos. 86 and 151 concerning migrant workers*. Geneva: International Labour Office, 1980.

International Labour Conference. 87th session, 1999. Report of the Committee of Experts on the Application of Conventions and Recommendations. *General Survey of the Reports relating to Conventions Nos. 97 and 143 and Recommendations Nos. 86 and 151 concerning migrant workers*. Geneva: International Labour Office, 1999.

Kapuy, Klaus. "Social security and the European Convention on Human Rights: How an odd couple has become presentable." *European Journal of Social Security* 3 (2007): 221–242.

Kapuy, Klaus, Danny Pieters and Bernhard Zaglmayer. *Social security cases in Europe: The European Court of Human Rights*. Antwerp/Oxford: Intersentia, 2007.

Mikkola, Matti. "Social human rights of migrants under the European Social Charter." *European Journal of Social Security* 1 (2008): 25–59.

Nußberger, Angelika. "Interpretation of international social security standards: Problems and prospects." In *International social security standards: Current views and interpretation matters*, edited by Frans Pennings, 33–50. Antwerp/Oxford: Intersentia, 2007.

Pieters, Danny. *Social Security: An introduction to the basic principles*. 2. edition. Alphen aan den Rijn: Kluwer Law International, 2006.

Schoukens, Paul. "Recht op gezondheidszorg volgens het internationale socialezekerheidsrecht." *Tijdschrift voor gezondheidsrecht* 2 (2008/2009): 96–115.

Schoukens, Paul and Danny Pieters. *Exploratory Report on the access to social protection for illegal labour migrants*. Strasbourg: Council of Europe, 2004.

Tiburcio, Carmen. *The human rights of aliens under international and comparative law*. The Hague/Boston/London: Martinus Nijhoff Publishers, 2001.

UN Commission on Human Rights, Sub-Commission on Prevention of Discrimination and Protection of Minorities. *International provisions protecting the human rights of non-citizens*. Study prepared by Baroness Elles, Special Rapporteur, UN Doc. E/CN.4/Sub.2/392/Rev.I (1980) I. New York: United Nations, 1980.

Vanheule, Dirk, Marie-Claire Foblets, Sander Loones and Steven Bouckaert. "De betekenis van de V.N.-Arbeidsmigrantenconventie van 18 december 1990 in het geval van ratificatie door België." In *Journal des tribunaux du travail* 894 (2004), 341–358.

Verscheuren, Herwig. "Toegang tot minimumvoorzieningen voor mensen zonder papieren: Een aftasten van de grenzen van het Europees recht." In *Tijdschrift voor sociaal recht* 4 (2005), 731–782.

Vonk, Gijsbert. "Migration, social security and the law: Some European dilemmas." In *European Journal of Social Security* 4 (2002), 315–332.

Vonk, Gijsbert and Klaus Kapuy. "Three approaches to refunding social insurance contributions to temporary migrant workers: Is there an attractive policy alternative?" In *European Journal of Social Security* 3 (2008), 227–247.

www.ingramcontent.com/pod-product-compliance
Ingram Content Group UK Ltd.
Pitfield, Milton Keynes, MK11 3LW, UK
UKHW051927100926
8556IPUK00022B/1426

9 789050 959414